DR. SHARON FORDE-ATIKOSSIE

STUDY THE
HOLY
BIBLE
IN ONE YEAR

(VOLUME 1)

CITI OF
BOOKS

CITIOFBOOKS, INC.
3736 Eubank NE Suite A1
Albuquerque, NM 87111-3579
www.citiofbooks.com
Hotline: 1 (877) 389-2759
Fax: 1 (505) 930-7244

Ordering Information:

Quantity sales. Special discounts are available on quantity purchases by corporations, associations, and others. For details, contact the publisher at the address above.

Printed in the United States of America.

ISBN-13:   Softcover   979-8-89391-694-2
                eBook   979-8-89391-695-9

Library of Congress Control Number: 2025909836

Table of Contents

All In One Inclusive Package

Volume I - I

Reading the Holy Bible in One year

Great book while travelling

This book gives you the opportunity to read and study the Holy Bible with ease, especially in places where bibles are not welcomed.

You have the opportunity to compare both Old and New Testament together from the beginning to the end.

From the Old Testament what was said and prophesy to the New Testament of Jesus Christ.

It gives one the opportunity to better understand the Holy Bible.

You are invited to read and study the Holy Bible within one year, or better yet, just take your time and read and study.

Many people have various ways to understand the Bible. Some read, some listen, and some does both, which is reading and listening at the same time.

Listening allows one to understand the pronunciation of many words. This procedure allows one to eliminate the distraction when reading it. (In some cases when one is reading the Bible, and they get stuck on words that they cannot pronounce, and when not understand the meaning of the word, they would become discourage, and just simply put the bible down)

Reading the Bible within one year means just reading the Bible not studying the Bible.

It takes time to actually read the bible, and it takes far longer if one wants read and study in the Bible at the same time.

When you look at the 1st chapter of the New Testament which is Matthew chapter 1 together the Book of Genisis one, two and three; you will see the tremendous amount of information that one has to cover, which includes the many biblical names.

This is the initial groundwork to reading and studying the bible.

Reading through the Bible within one Year

The Holy Bible is a sacred book that contains the word of God. Throughout its pages, the Holy Bible teaches that God never stops loving His children, and there are many reasons for its existence, including:

To teach God's will

The Bible is a guidebook for life, teaching how to live, how to deal with difficult situations, and how to have a relationship with God.

To reveal God's plan of salvation

The Bible shows God's plan of salvation for humanity and how to deal with sin.

To strengthen endurance

The Bible can help people endure suffering, trials, and losses, and to keep trusting and worshiping the Lord.

To glorify God

The Bible is about what God has done to redeem his people, judge sin, and make all things new in Christ.

To confirm the word of God

Christians believe that Jesus confirmed the Old Testament scriptures as the written word of God and the ultimate authority in life.

In each section of the Bible, we see God's holy, unchanging, faithful, gracious and loving character.

The Bible tells us in 2 Timothy 3:16–17 when discussing the topic of Scripture says that it is "profitable for teaching, for reproof, for correction and for training in righteousness."

The next verse goes on to say that this leads to the completeness and equipping "for every good work" (ESV).

Regularly reading God's word reorients our thinking so that we can grow in maturity, which is part of the Christian calling (Ephesians 4:14–16; Romans 12:1–2).

Have you ever met a mature Christian who did not regularly read the Bible?

These three things are really just the beginning, this list could include dozens of reasons why you should read the Bible on a regular basis.

How to read

Note... The Bible is not just a one time read, it must be read regularly, daily if possible.

There are many suggestions on how to read the bible.

It is recommended to read Both Old Testament and New Testament together in order to understand how both books coincide with each other.

If you're new at reading the Bible, it is suggested to start with the first four books of the New Testament and in the old testament Genisis.

It is best to always have a bible reading plan

It is advised to take it slow, since while reading there are many reference area in the bible.

Always seek guidance from your pastor.

From experience reading the bible from Genesis to revelation without writing notes, was fruitless. I retained nothing, and everything seemed confusing.

I got a better understanding after getting using a plan, and read it daily.

Bible teaches about Jesus

Jesus Christ is God's Son who came to earth to save us from sin, sadness, loneliness, pain, and more. Jesus taught beautiful lessons about service and love and performed many miracles while He was on earth. In the Bible, we can read these stories and begin to know how we can overcome hard things with help from Jesus.

It's here to help

Following the teachings found in the Bible helps us to know who God is, learn from good people who loved Him, and better understand how He wants us to live.

This book was prepared for various reasons

In many countries the Holy Bible is not permitted to read outside. If caught, there is either, a fine or punishment, especially in countries where the bible is forbidden to read.

The bible is distinctive, and can be recognized everywhere, regardless of its cover

Many people are intimidated by the bible, and they are afraid to open and read it, especially in public.

Having this book in this form, allow you to read with ease, and also, able to write your notes.

The Holy Bible is a very respectable book, and most people do not want to take it out of their home, but having this book in their bags or have it anywhere.

These are the collective chapters when reading and researching the Holy Bible.

Having the opportunity to read the bible and also studying the bible over, and over, it give me many insight, and I am still in awe at how much I have not grasped.

In most cases it would create about three years to actually get the real concept, and in-depth studying would take about five to ten years with at least four hours daily, and to be honest after studying there are still a lot mor to learn.

Every time I pick up the bible there is always something I have missed or breezed over.

As a missionary, I am always reading the bible and this is for two reasons, and that is learn more, and the other is to prepare myself for what is to come, while on mission trips.

Dr. Sharon Forde-Atikossie

Tools needed

Pen, marker and yourself

Select a specific time to read or study

Select a quiet place to ready and study

Pray and ask God to bring everything into clarity

Read through the chapters first

Re-read the bible verses thoroughly

Compare the Old Testament and new testaments

Recommend reading in chronological order to get a better understanding

VOLUME I
MONTH ONE
DAY 1 OF DAY 31

Chapters in the Bible to read

Matthew Chapter 1

Genesis 1

Genesis 2

Genesis 3

Bible commentaries

SUMMARY OF MATTHEW 1

Matthew tells the good news

Matthew chapter 1 serves as the introduction to the Gospel of Matthew, establishing key themes, and providing essential background information about Jesus Christ.

Here are the main components and their meanings:

The purpose of this chapter shows the genealogy traces Jesus' lineage back to Abraham, emphasizing His Jewish heritage and fulfilling Old Testament prophecies regarding the Messiah's descent from David.

It is divided into three groups of fourteen generations, highlighting God's providence and the significance of numbers in biblical texts.

The figures in this chapter includes the inclusion of women like Tamar, Rahab, Ruth, and Bathsheba illustrates God's grace, and the breaking of social norms.

It tells of the Birth of Jesus, showing the announcement of Mary's Pregnancy where it describes how Mary was found to be with child by the Holy Spirit before she and Joseph came together, emphasizing the miraculous nature of Jesus' birth.

It also explained Joseph's dilemma where Joseph's initial plan to divorce Mary quietly reflects his righteousness and compassion. An angel's message reassures him, stressing the importance of Jesus' mission, and the fulfillment of prophecy which links Jesus' birth to prophetic fulfillment, specifically that He would be called "Immanuel," meaning "God with us."

BOOK MATTHEW CHAPTER 1
KING JAMES VERSION

¹ The book of the generation of Jesus Christ, the son of David, the son of Abraham.

² Abraham begat Isaac; and Isaac begat Jacob; and Jacob begat Judas and his brethren;

³ And Judas begat Phares and Zara of Thamar; and Phares begat Esrom; and Esrom begat Aram;

⁴ And Aram begat Aminadab; and Aminadab begat Naasson; and Naasson begat Salmon;

⁵ And Salmon begat Booz of Rachab; and Booz begat Obed of Ruth; and Obed begat Jesse;

⁶ And Jesse begat David the king; and David the king begat Solomon of her that had been the wife of Urias;

⁷ And Solomon begat Roboam; and Roboam begat Abia; and Abia begat Asa;

⁸ And Asa begat Josaphat; and Josaphat begat Joram; and Joram begat Ozias;

⁹ And Ozias begat Joatham; and Joatham begat Achaz; and Achaz begat Ezekias;

¹⁰ And Ezekias begat Manasses; and Manasses begat Amon; and Amon begat Josias;

¹¹ And Josias begat Jechonias and his brethren, about the time they were carried away to Babylon:

¹² And after they were brought to Babylon, Jechonias begat Salathiel; and Salathiel begat Zorobabel;

¹³ And Zorobabel begat Abiud; and Abiud begat Eliakim; and Eliakim begat Azor;

¹⁴ And Azor begat Sadoc; and Sadoc begat Achim; and Achim begat Eliud;

¹⁵ And Eliud begat Eleazar; and Eleazar begat Matthan; and Matthan begat Jacob;

¹⁶ And Jacob begat Joseph the husband of Mary, of whom was born Jesus, who is called Christ.

¹⁷ So all the generations from Abraham to David are fourteen generations; and from David until the carrying away into Babylon are fourteen generations; and from the carrying away into Babylon unto Christ are fourteen generations.

¹⁸ Now the birth of Jesus Christ was on this wise: When as his mother Mary was espoused to Joseph, before they came together, she was found with child of the Holy Ghost.

¹⁹ Then Joseph her husband, being a just man, and not willing to make her a public example, was minded to put her away privily.

²⁰ But while he thought on these things, behold, the angel of the Lord appeared unto him in a dream, saying, Joseph, thou son of David, fear not to take unto thee Mary thy wife: for that which is conceived in her is of the Holy Ghost.

²¹ And she shall bring forth a son, and thou shalt call his name Jesus: for he shall save his people from their sins.

²² Now all this was done, that it might be fulfilled which was spoken of the Lord by the prophet, saying,

²³ Behold, a virgin shall be with child, and shall bring forth a son, and they shall call his name Emmanuel, which being interpreted is, God with us.

²⁴ Then Joseph being raised from sleep did as the angel of the Lord had bidden him, and took unto him his wife:

²⁵ And knew her not till she had brought forth her firstborn son: and he called his name Jesus.

Footnotes

a. Matthew 1:1 Or is an account of the origin

b. Matthew 1:1 Or Jesus Christ. Messiah (Hebrew) and Christ (Greek) both mean Anointed One; also in verse 18.

c. Matthew 1:11 That is, Jehoiachin; also in verse 12

d. Matthew 1:18 Or The origin of Jesus the Messiah was like this

e. Matthew 1:19 Or was a righteous man and

f. Matthew 1:21 Jesus is the Greek form of Joshua, which means the Lord saves.

g. Matthew 1:23 Isaiah 7:14

GENESIS 1

King James Version

1 In the beginning God created the heaven and the earth.

² And the earth was without form, and void; and darkness was upon the face of the deep. And the Spirit of God moved upon the face of the waters.

³ And God said, Let there be light: and there was light.

⁴ And God saw the light, that it was good: and God divided the light from the darkness.

⁵ And God called the light Day, and the darkness he called Night. And the evening and the morning were the first day.

⁶ And God said, Let there be a firmament in the midst of the waters, and let it divide the waters from the waters.

⁷ And God made the firmament, and divided the waters which were under the firmament from the waters which were above the firmament: and it was so.

⁸ And God called the firmament Heaven. And the evening and the morning were the second day.

⁹ And God said, Let the waters under the heaven be gathered together unto one place, and let the dry land appear: and it was so.

[10] And God called the dry land Earth; and the gathering together of the waters called he Seas: and God saw that it was good.

[11] And God said, Let the earth bring forth grass, the herb yielding seed, and the fruit tree yielding fruit after his kind, whose seed is in itself, upon the earth: and it was so.

[12] And the earth brought forth grass, and herb yielding seed after his kind, and the tree yielding fruit, whose seed was in itself, after his kind: and God saw that it was good.

[13] And the evening and the morning were the third day.

[14] And God said, Let there be lights in the firmament of the heaven to divide the day from the night; and let them be for signs, and for seasons, and for days, and years:

[15] And let them be for lights in the firmament of the heaven to give light upon the earth: and it was so.

[16] And God made two great lights; the greater light to rule the day, and the lesser light to rule the night: he made the stars also.

[17] And God set them in the firmament of the heaven to give light upon the earth,

[18] And to rule over the day and over the night, and to divide the light from the darkness: and God saw that it was good.

[19] And the evening and the morning were the fourth day.

20 And God said, Let the waters bring forth abundantly the moving creature that hath life, and fowl that may fly above the earth in the open firmament of heaven.

21 And God created great whales, and every living creature that moveth, which the waters brought forth abundantly, after their kind, and every winged fowl after his kind: and God saw that it was good.

22 And God blessed them, saying, Be fruitful, and multiply, and fill the waters in the seas, and let fowl multiply in the earth.

23 And the evening and the morning were the fifth day.

24 And God said, Let the earth bring forth the living creature after his kind, cattle, and creeping thing, and beast of the earth after his kind: and it was so.

25 And God made the beast of the earth after his kind, and cattle after their kind, and every thing that creepeth upon the earth after his kind: and God saw that it was good.

26 And God said, Let us make man in our image, after our likeness: and let them have dominion over the fish of the sea, and over the fowl of the air, and over the cattle, and over all the earth, and over every creeping thing that creepeth upon the earth.

27 So God created man in his own image, in the image of God created he him; male and female created he them.

28 And God blessed them, and God said unto them, Be fruitful, and multiply, and replenish the earth, and subdue it: and have dominion over the fish of the sea,

and over the fowl of the air, and over every living thing that moveth upon the earth.

[29] And God said, Behold, I have given you every herb bearing seed, which is upon the face of all the earth, and every tree, in the which is the fruit of a tree yielding seed; to you it shall be for meat.

[30] And to every beast of the earth, and to every fowl of the air, and to every thing that creepeth upon the earth, wherein there is life, I have given every green herb for meat: and it was so.

[31] And God saw every thing that he had made, and, behold, it was very good. And the evening and the morning were the sixth day.

GENESIS 2

King James Version

2 Thus the heavens and the earth were finished, and all the host of them.

² And on the seventh day God ended his work which he had made; and he rested on the seventh day from all his work which he had made.

³ And God blessed the seventh day, and sanctified it: because that in it he had rested from all his work which God created and made.

⁴ These are the generations of the heavens and of the earth when they were created, in the day that the Lord God made the earth and the heavens,

⁵ And every plant of the field before it was in the earth, and every herb of the field before it grew: for the Lord God had not caused it to rain upon the earth, and there was not a man to till the ground.

⁶ But there went up a mist from the earth, and watered the whole face of the ground.

⁷ And the Lord God formed man of the dust of the ground, and breathed into his nostrils the breath of life; and man became a living soul.

⁸ And the Lord God planted a garden eastward in Eden; and there he put the man whom he had formed.

⁹ And out of the ground made the Lord God to grow every tree that is pleasant to the sight, and good for food; the tree of life also in the midst of the garden, and the tree of knowledge of good and evil.

¹⁰ And a river went out of Eden to water the garden; and from thence it was parted, and became into four heads.

¹¹ The name of the first is Pison: that is it which compasseth the whole land of Havilah, where there is gold;

¹² And the gold of that land is good: there is bdellium and the onyx stone.

¹³ And the name of the second river is Gihon: the same is it that compasseth the whole land of Ethiopia.

¹⁴ And the name of the third river is Hiddekel: that is it which goeth toward the east of Assyria. And the fourth river is Euphrates.

¹⁵ And the Lord God took the man, and put him into the garden of Eden to dress it and to keep it.

¹⁶ And the Lord God commanded the man, saying, Of every tree of the garden thou mayest freely eat:

¹⁷ But of the tree of the knowledge of good and evil, thou shalt not eat of it: for in the day that thou eatest thereof thou shalt surely die.

¹⁸ And the Lord God said, It is not good that the man should be alone; I will make him an help meet for him.

¹⁹ And out of the ground the Lord God formed every beast of the field, and every fowl of the air; and brought

them unto Adam to see what he would call them: and whatsoever Adam called every living creature, that was the name thereof.

²⁰ And Adam gave names to all cattle, and to the fowl of the air, and to every beast of the field; but for Adam there was not found an help meet for him.

²¹ And the Lord God caused a deep sleep to fall upon Adam, and he slept: and he took one of his ribs, and closed up the flesh instead thereof;

Study of the Holy Bible in One Year (Volume 1)

²² And the rib, which the Lord God had taken from man, made he a woman, and brought her unto the man.

²³ And Adam said, This is now bone of my bones, and flesh of my flesh: she shall be called Woman, because she was taken out of Man.

²⁴ Therefore shall a man leave his father and his mother, and shall cleave unto his wife: and they shall be one flesh.

²⁵ And they were both naked, the man and his wife, and were not ashamed.

GENESIS 3

King James Version

3 Now the serpent was more subtil than any beast of the field which the Lord God had made. And he said unto the woman, Yea, hath God said, Ye shall not eat of every tree of the garden?

² And the woman said unto the serpent, We may eat of the fruit of the trees of the garden:

³ But of the fruit of the tree which is in the midst of the garden, God hath said, Ye shall not eat of it, neither shall ye touch it, lest ye die.

⁴ And the serpent said unto the woman, Ye shall not surely die:

⁵ For God doth know that in the day ye eat thereof, then your eyes shall be opened, and ye shall be as gods, knowing good and evil.

⁶ And when the woman saw that the tree was good for food, and that it was pleasant to the eyes, and a tree to be desired to make one wise, she took of the fruit thereof, and did eat, and gave also unto her husband with her; and he did eat.

⁷ And the eyes of them both were opened, and they knew that they were naked; and they sewed fig leaves together, and made themselves aprons.

⁸ And they heard the voice of the Lord God walking in the garden in the cool of the day: and Adam and his wife hid themselves from the presence of the Lord God amongst the trees of the garden.

⁹ And the Lord God called unto Adam, and said unto him, Where art thou?

¹⁰ And he said, I heard thy voice in the garden, and I was afraid, because I was naked; and I hid myself.

¹¹ And he said, Who told thee that thou wast naked? Hast thou eaten of the tree, whereof I commanded thee that thou shouldest not eat?

¹² And the man said, The woman whom thou gavest to be with me, she gave me of the tree, and I did eat.

¹³ And the Lord God said unto the woman, What is this that thou hast done? And the woman said, The serpent beguiled me, and I did eat.

¹⁴ And the Lord God said unto the serpent, Because thou hast done this, thou art cursed above all cattle, and above every beast of the field; upon thy belly shalt thou go, and dust shalt thou eat all the days of thy life:

¹⁵ And I will put enmity between thee and the woman, and between thy seed and her seed; it shall bruise thy head, and thou shalt bruise his heel.

¹⁶ Unto the woman he said, I will greatly multiply thy sorrow and thy conception; in sorrow thou shalt bring forth children; and thy desire shall be to thy husband, and he shall rule over thee.

¹⁷ And unto Adam he said, Because thou hast hearkened unto the voice of thy wife, and hast eaten of the tree,

of which I commanded thee, saying, Thou shalt not eat of it: cursed is the ground for thy sake; in sorrow shalt thou eat of it all the days of thy life;

[18] Thorns also and thistles shall it bring forth to thee; and thou shalt eat the herb of the field;

[19] In the sweat of thy face shalt thou eat bread, till thou return unto the ground; for out of it wast thou taken: for dust thou art, and unto dust shalt thou return.

[20] And Adam called his wife's name Eve; because she was the mother of all living.

[21] Unto Adam also and to his wife did the Lord God make coats of skins, and clothed them.

[22] And the Lord God said, Behold, the man is become as one of us, to know good and evil: and now, lest he put forth his hand, and take also of the tree of life, and eat, and live for ever:

[23] Therefore the Lord God sent him forth from the garden of Eden, to till the ground from whence he was taken.

[24] So he drove out the man; and he placed at the east of the garden of Eden Cherubims, and a flaming sword which turned every way, to keep the way of the tree of life.

BIBLE COMMENTARY

Matthew 1 – Genealogy, Origins, History

The Genealogy of Jesus Christ.

1. (1) Matthew presents his theme in the first verse: Jesus as the fulfillment of prophecy and of Israel's expectation.

The book of the genealogy of Jesus Christ, the Son of David, the Son of Abraham:

a. The book of the genealogy of Jesus Christ: So, Matthew begins his account of the life of Jesus Christ. From the statement in the ancient Greek text, it is difficult to tell what the book of the genealogy refers to.

i. "The first two words of Matthew, biblos genseos, may be translated 'record of the genealogy,' 'record of the origins,' or 'record of the history'" (Carson). There is a sense in which each meaning is valid.

In Matthew 1:1-17 we have the "record of the genealogy."

In Matthew 1:18-2:23 we have the "record of the origins."

In the entire Gospel of Matthew we have the "record of the history."

ii. As a former tax collector (also called "Levi"), Matthew was qualified to write an account of Jesus' life and teachings. A tax collector of that day must know Greek and be a literate, well-organized man. Some think that Matthew was the "recorder" among the disciples and took notes of Jesus' teaching. We might say that when Matthew followed Jesus, he left everything behind – except his pen and paper. "Matthew nobly used his literary skill to become the first man ever to compile an account of the teaching of Jesus." (Barclay)

iii. "We know that he was a tax-gatherer and that he must therefore have been a bitterly hated man, for the Jews hated the members of their own race who had entered the civil service of their conquerors." (Barclay)

b. The Son of David, the Son of Abraham: In this overview of explaining the lineage of Jesus, Matthew clearly and strongly connects him to some of the greatest men in the history of the Old Testament. Matthew begins his account of the life of Jesus Christ with the record of the lineage of Jesus from the patriarch Abraham.

i. Though most New Testament scholars believe that the Gospel of Matthew was not the first of the four written, it is well placed as the first book of the New Testament. There are many reasons why Matthew belongs first among the gospel accounts.

"It is a remarkable fact that, among the variations in the order in which the Gospels appear in early lists and texts, the one constant factor is that Matthew always comes first."

In the early days of Christianity, many people thought that the Gospel of Matthew was the first written.

The early Christians rightly saw the Gospel of Matthew as important because it has some significant portions of Jesus' teaching that are not included in other gospels, such as a fuller version of the Sermon on the Mount.

It was the only one of the synoptic gospels (Matthew, Mark, and Luke) to have an apostolic author – Matthew (who was also known as Levi), who was a former tax collector before he followed Jesus as a disciple.

"Matthew's Gospel was in fact far more quoted in Christian writings of the second Christian century than any other."

The Jewish flavor of the Gospel of Matthew makes for a logical transition between the Old and New Testaments. For these reasons, the early church placed it first in order among the four gospel accounts.

ii. The Jewish character of this Gospel is evident in many ways. There are many indications that Matthew expected that his readers would be familiar with Jewish culture.

Matthew doesn't translate Aramaic terms such as raca (Matthew 5:22) and corban (Matthew 15:5).

Matthew refers to Jewish customs without explanation (Matthew 15:2 to Mark 4-7:3; see also Matthew 23:5).

Matthew starts his genealogy with Abraham (Matthew 1:1).

Matthew presents the name of Jesus and its meaning in a way that assumes the reader knows its Hebrew roots (Matthew 1:21).

Matthew frequently refers to Jesus as the "Son of David."

Matthew uses the more Jewish phrase "Kingdom of Heaven" instead of "Kingdom of God."

iii. Yet significantly, the Gospel of Matthew also triumphantly ends with Jesus commanding His followers to make disciples of all the nations (Matthew 28:19-20). So the Gospel of Matthew is deeply rooted in Judaism, but at the same time is able to look beyond; it sees the gospel itself as more than a message for the Jewish people; rather it is a message for the whole world.

iv. We also see that Matthew is deeply critical of the Jewish leadership and their rejection of Jesus. To say that Matthew is "pro-Jewish" is incorrect; it is better to say that he is "pro-Jesus," and presents Jesus as the authentic Jewish Messiah, whom sadly many of the Jewish people (especially the religious establishment) rejected.

v. Some early church commentators and modern scholars say that Matthew originally wrote his gospel in Hebrew, and it was then translated into Greek. Yet there is no concrete evidence for this theory, such as the discovery of an early Hebrew manuscript of Matthew.

vi. More modern theories about the Gospel of Matthew say that he wrote in the style of Jewish midrash literature, which creates imaginary stories as a running commentary on the Old Testament. Certain writers use the midrash example to say that Matthew wrote about many events that never happened, but he wasn't lying because he never intended to tell the truth, and his audience never believed that he was.

These are unconvincing theories, and analysis shows more differences than similarities between Matthew and midrashim. "Jewish Midrashim...present stories as illustrative material by way of commenting on a running Old Testament text. By contrast Matthew 1-2 offers no running Old Testament text." (Carson)

c. Son of David: Throughout his work, Matthew presents Jesus as the kingly Messiah promised from David's royal line (2 Samuel 7:12-16).

i. The Old Testament prophesied that the Messiah would be the Son of David; in the very first sentence, Matthew points to Jesus as the fulfillment of Old Testament prophecy.

d. Son of Abraham: Matthew not only connected Jesus to David, but back yet further to Abraham. Jesus is the Seed of Abraham in whom all nations would be blessed (Genesis 12:3).

2. (2-16) Jesus' Genealogy through Joseph.

Abraham begot Isaac, Isaac begot Jacob, and Jacob begot Judah and his brothers. Judah begot Perez and Zerah by Tamar, Perez begot Hezron, and Hezron begot Ram. Ram begot Amminadab, Amminadab begot Nahshon, and Nahshon begot Salmon. Salmon begot Boaz by Rahab, Boaz begot Obed by Ruth, Obed begot Jesse, and Jesse begot David the king. David the king begot Solomon by her who had been the wife of Uriah. Solomon begot Rehoboam, Rehoboam begot Abijah, and Abijah begot Asa. Asa begot Jehoshaphat, Jehoshaphat begot Joram, and Joram begot Uzziah. Uzziah begot Jotham, Jotham begot Ahaz, and Ahaz begot Hezekiah. Hezekiah begot Manasseh, Manasseh begot Amon, and Amon begot Josiah. Josiah begot Jeconiah and his brothers about the time they were carried away to Babylon. And after they were brought to Babylon, Jeconiah begot Shealtiel, and Shealtiel begot Zerubbabel. Zerubbabel begot Abiud, Abiud begot Eliakim, and Eliakim begot Azor. Azor begot Zadok, Zadok begot Achim, and Achim begot Eliud. Eliud begot Eleazar, Eleazar begot Matthan, and Matthan begot Jacob. And Jacob begot Joseph the husband of Mary, of whom was born Jesus who is called Christ.

a. Abraham… Joseph: This genealogy establishes Jesus' claim to the throne of David through his adoptive father Joseph. This is not the blood lineage of Jesus through Mary, but the legal lineage of Jesus through Joseph. The Gospel of Luke provides Jesus' blood lineage through Mary.

i. "The Jews set much store by genealogies, and to Jewish Christians the Messiahship of Jesus depended on its being proved that he was a descendant of David." (Bruce)

ii. There are some genuine problems in sorting out the details of this genealogy and reconciling some points to both Luke's record and those found in the Old Testament.

iii. The author is persuaded that Matthew records the genealogical record of Joseph, and Luke the record of Mary; but this is not accepted without dispute by some. "Few would guess simply by reading Luke that he is giving Mary's genealogy. The theory stems, not from the text of Luke, but from the need to harmonize the two genealogies. On the face of it, both Matthew and Luke aim to give Joseph's genealogy." (Carson)

iv. Nevertheless, genealogical difficulties should not prevent us from seeing the whole. Matthew Poole acknowledged that there were some problems with the genealogies, and in reconciling the records of Matthew and Luke, yet he rightly observed:

The Jews kept extensive genealogical records, and so it is not unwise to trust such records.

We should remember Paul's warnings about striving over genealogies and not get into arguments about them (1 Timothy 1:4 and 6:4; Titus 3:9).

If the Jewish opponents of Jesus could have demonstrated that He was not descended from David, they would have disqualified His claim to be Messiah; yet they did not and could not.

"And therefore it is the most unreasonable thing imaginable for us to make such little dissatisfactions grounds for us to question or disbelieve the gospel, because we cannot untie every knot we meet with in a pedigree." (Poole)

vi. The Jewish interest in genealogies could sometimes be a dangerous distraction. Therefore Paul warned Timothy to guard against those who were fascinated by endless genealogies (1 Timothy 1:4), and he gave a similar warning to Titus (Titus 3:9).

vii. "With one or two exceptions these are the names of persons of little or no note. The later ones were persons altogether obscure and insignificant. Our Lord was 'a root out of dry ground'; a shoot from a withered stem of Jesse. He set small store by earthly greatness." (Spurgeon)

b. Tamar... Rahab... Ruth... her who had been the wife of Uriah: This genealogy is noted for the unusual presence of four women. Women were rarely mentioned in ancient genealogies, and the four mentioned here are worthy of special note as examples of God's grace. They show how God can take unlikely people and use them in great ways.

Tamar: She sold herself as a prostitute to her fatherin-law Judah to bring forth Perez and Zerah (Genesis 38).

Rahab: She was a Gentile prostitute, for whom God took extraordinary measures to save from both judgment and her lifestyle of prostitution (Joshua 2; 6:22-23).

Ruth: She was from Moab, a Gentile, and outside of the covenant of Israel until her conversion (Ruth 1).

Her who had been the wife of Uriah: Bathsheba (who is mentioned by implication in Matthew 1:6) was an adulteress, infamous for her sin with David (2 Samuel 11.) "Matthew's peculiar way of referring to her, 'Uriah's wife,' may be an attempt to focus on the fact that Uriah was not an Israelite but a Hittite." (Carson)

i. These four women have an important place in the genealogy of Jesus to demonstrate that Jesus Christ was not royalty according to human perception in the sense that He did not come from a pure aristocratic background.

ii. These four women have an important place in the genealogy of Jesus to demonstrate that Jesus identifies with sinners in His genealogy, even as He will in His birth, baptism, life, and His death on the cross. "Jesus is heir of a line in which flows the blood of the harlot Rahab, and of the rustic Ruth; he is akin to the fallen and to the lowly, and he will show his love even to the poorest and most obscure." (Spurgeon)

iii. These four women have an important place in the genealogy of Jesus to show that there is a new place for women under the New Covenant. In both the pagan and the Jewish culture of that day, men often had little regard for women. In that era, some Jewish men prayed every morning thanking God that they were not Gentiles, slaves or women. Despite that, women were regarded more highly among the Jews than they were among the pagans.

iv. "By far the most amazing thing about this pedigree is the names of the women who appear in it." (Barclay)

v. "Men and women, notorious for their evil character, lie in the direct line of his descent. This was permitted, that He might fully represent our fallen race." (Meyer)

c. Jacob begot Joseph the husband of Mary, of whom was born Jesus who is called Christ: Matthew wanted to make it clear that Joseph was not the father of Jesus; rather he was the husband of Mary.

i. "The new phraseology makes it clear that Matthew does not regard Jesus as Joseph's son physically…The genealogy is clearly intended to be that of Jesus' 'legal' ancestry, not of his physical descent." (France)

3. (17) Matthew's Organization of the Genealogy.

So all the generations from Abraham to David are fourteen generations, from David until the captivity in Babylon are fourteen generations, and from the captivity in Babylon until the Christ are fourteen generations.

a. Fourteen generations…fourteen generations… fourteen generations: Here Matthew made it clear that this genealogy is not complete. There were not actually fourteen generations between the points indicated, but Matthew edited the list to make it easy to remember and memorize.

i. For example, Matthew 1:8 says Joram begot Uzziah. This was Uzziah, King of Judah, who was struck with leprosy for daring to enter the temple as a priest to offer incense (2 Chronicles 21-26:16). Uzziah was not the immediate son of Joram; there were three kings between them (Ahaziah, Joash, and Amaziah). Yet as Clarke rightly says, "It is observed that omissions of this kind are not uncommon in the Jewish genealogies."

b. So all the generations: The practice of skipping generations at times was common in the listing of ancient genealogies. Matthew did nothing unusual by leaving some generations out.

i. .Another of the royal line that Matthew passed over was in between Josiah and Jechoniah (Matthew 1:11), and his name was Jehoakim (2 Chronicles -36:5 8). Jehoakim was so wicked that through the Prophet Jeremiah, God promised that no blood descendant of his would sit on the throne of Israel (Jeremiah 36:3031). This presented a significant problem: If someone was a blood descendant of David through Jehoakim, he could not sit on the throne of Israel and be the king and the Messiah because of this curse recorded in Jeremiah 36:30-31. But if the conqueror was not descended through David, he could not be the legal heir of the throne because of the promise made to David and the nature of the royal line.

ii. This is where we come to the differences in the genealogies of Matthew and Luke. Matthew recorded the genealogy of Joseph, the husband of Mary, of whom was born Jesus who is called Christ (Matthew 1:16). He began at Abraham and followed the line down to Jesus, through Joseph. Luke recorded the genealogy of Mary: being, (as was supposed) the son of Joseph (Luke 3:23). He began with Jesus and followed the line back up, all the way to Adam, starting from the unmentioned Mary.

iii. Each genealogy is the same as it records the line from Adam (or Abraham) all the way down to David. But at David, the two genealogies separated. If we remember the list of David's sons in 2 Samuel 5, we see that Satan focused his attention on the descendants of the royal line through Solomon – and this was a reasonable strategy. According to Matthew 1:6, Joseph's line went through Solomon (and therefore Jehoakim, the cursed one). Jesus was the legal son of Joseph, but not the blood son of Joseph – so the curse on Jehoakim did not affect him. Joseph did not contribute any of the "blood" of Jesus, but he did contribute his legal standing as a descendant of the royal line to Jesus.

Mary's line – the blood line of Jesus – did not go through Solomon, but through a different son of David, named Nathan (Luke 3:31). Mary was therefore not part of that blood curse on the line of Jehoiakim.

B. The Birth of Jesus Christ.

1. (18) Mary, while engaged to Joseph, is found to be with child as a result of a miraculous conception by the Holy Spirit.

Now the birth of Jesus Christ was as follows: After His mother Mary was betrothed to Joseph, before they came together, she was found with child of the Holy Spirit.

a. Now the birth of Jesus Christ was as follows: Matthew doesn't really tell us about the birth of Jesus; Luke does that. Matthew instead tells us where Jesus came from, and it tells the story through the eyes of Joseph.

b. After His mother Mary was betrothed to Joseph: There were essentially three steps to marriage in the Jewish world of Jesus' time.

Engagement: This could happen when the bride and groom to be were quite young, and was often arranged by the parents.

Betrothal: This made the previous engagement official and binding. During the time of betrothal the couple were known as husband and wife, and a betrothal could only be broken by divorce. Betrothal typically lasted a year.

Marriage: This took place after the wedding, after the year of betrothal.

c. She was found with child of the Holy Spirit: Matthew plainly (without the greater detail found in the Gospel of Luke) presents the virginal conception and subsequent birth of Jesus. However, the virgin birth was difficult for people to believe back then, even as it is also doubted now by some.

i. We should consider what a great trial this was for a godly young woman like Mary, and for Joseph her betrothed. "Her situation was the most distressing and humiliating that can be conceived. Nothing but the fullest consciousness of her own integrity, and the strongest confidence in God, could have supported her in such trying circumstances, where her reputation, her honor, and her life were at stake." (Clarke)

ii. The truth of the supernatural conception of Jesus was disbelieved by many then and was later twisted into lies about the parentage of Jesus. References are made to these suspicions in passages like John 8:19 and 8:41. Lies spread that Mary had become pregnant from a Roman soldier. Here, Matthew set the story straight – both then and now.

iii. "There was no other way of his being born; for had he been of a sinful father, how should he have possessed a sinless nature? He is born of a woman, that he might be human; but not by man, that he might not be sinful." (Spurgeon)

2. (19) Joseph seeks a quiet divorce.

Then Joseph her husband, being a just man, and not wanting to make her a public example, was minded to put her away secretly.

a. Joseph her husband: The previous verse told us that Mary was betrothed to Joseph. This comment shows that even though they were not formally married, Joseph was still considered Mary's husband by betrothal.

b. Being a just man, and not wanting to make her a public example: Being a just man, Joseph knew that if Mary had been unfaithful to him it would be impossible to go through with the marriage. Yet his nature as a just man also did not want to make this an unnecessary hardship or stigma upon Mary. Joseph made the understandable decision to seek a quiet divorce.

c. To put her away secretly: This refers to breaking an engagement by divorce. In Jewish culture of that time, a betrothal was binding and one needed a divorce to break the arrangement.

i. "Their being betrothed was a thing publicly taken notice of, and he could not put her away so privately but there must be witnesses of it; the meaning therefore must be, as privately as the nature of thing would bear." (Poole)

ii. "When we have to do a severe thing, let us choose the tenderest manner. Maybe we shall not have to do it at all." (Spurgeon)

3. (20-21) An angel speaks to Joseph in a dream, convincing him not to divorce Mary.

But while he thought about these things, behold, an angel of the Lord appeared to him in a dream, saying, "Joseph, son of David, do not be afraid to take to you Mary your wife, for that which is conceived in her is of the Holy Spirit. And she will bring forth a Son, and you shall call His name JESUS, for He will save His people from their sins."

a. Behold, an angel of the Lord appeared to him in a dream: This was not the Angel of the LORD, but simply an angel of the Lord. Perhaps it was Gabriel, who is prominent in the announcements made to Mary and Zacharias (Luke 1:19 and 1:26). Yet those were actual angelic visitations; this was presented to Joseph in a dream.

i. The dream came while he thought about these things. Joseph was understandably troubled by Mary's mysterious pregnancy, her future, and what he should do towards her. Though he had decided to put her away secretly, he was not comfortable with that decision.

b. Joseph, son of David: The address son of David should have alerted Joseph that something was particularly significant about this message. Son of David is a reference to Joseph's legal lineage to the throne of David.

c. That which is conceived in her is of the Holy Spirit: It seems that Mary had not told Joseph that she was pregnant by the Holy Spirit. This shouldn't surprise us; how could she (or how could anyone except God) explain such a thing? This angelic word to Joseph was persuasive.

i. There is no explanation as to how this happened, other than what we have in Luke 1:35. "This wonderful conception of our Saviour is a mystery not much to be pried into, and is therefore called an overshadowing, Luke 1:35." (Trapp)

ii. "There is no hint of pagan deity-human coupling in crassly physical terms. Instead, the power of the Lord, manifest in the Holy Spirit who was expected to be active in the Messianic Age, miraculously brought about the conception."

d. You shall call his name JESUS: The name JESUS ("The Salvation of Yahweh") was fairly common in that day (Josephus mentions 12 different men named "Jesus" in his writings), but it is supremely blessed in our day. As was later said by the Apostle Peter, there is no other name under heaven by which men must be saved (Acts 4:12).

i. "The name which the angel commanded Joseph to give to Mary's Child was one that was common at the time…its full significance was 'The Salvation of Jehovah.'" (Morgan)

e. For He will save His people from their sins: The angelic messenger briefly and eloquently stated the work of the coming Messiah, Jesus. He will come as a savior, and come to save His people from their sins.

i. This description of the work of Jesus reminds us that Jesus meets us in our sin, but His purpose is to save us from our sins. He saves us first from the penalty of sin, then from the power of sin, and finally from the presence of sin.

ii. "Salvation from sins is an element in the Old Testament hope (e.g. Isaiah 53; Jeremiah 31:31-34; Ezekiel 36:24-31) and in later Messianic expectation... but not the dominant one. Its isolation here warns the reader not to expect this Messiah to conform to the more popular hope of a national liberator."

iii. Wonderfully, it says "His people." If it had said, "God's people," we might have thought it was reserved for the Jewish people alone. But it isn't belonging to Abraham that brings salvation from sin; it is belonging to Jesus, being one of His people.

4. (22-23) The virgin birth as the fulfillment of prophecy.

So all this was done that it might be fulfilled which was spoken by the Lord through the prophet, saying: "Behold, the virgin shall be with child, and bear a Son, and they shall call His name Immanuel," which is translated, "God with us."

a. That it might be fulfilled: This is the first use of this important phrase which will become a familiar theme throughout Matthew.

b. "Behold, the virgin shall be with child, and bear a Son, and they shall call His name Immanuel": Matthew rightly understood that the supernatural conception of Jesus was prophesied in Isaiah 7:14.

i. There has been some measure of controversy regarding this quote from Isaiah 7:14, primarily because the Hebrew word almah can be translated as either virgin or "young woman."

ii. We know the Isaiah passage speaks of Jesus because it says the virgin shall be with child, and that conception would be a sign to David's entire house. Those who deny the virgin birth of Jesus like to point out that the Hebrew word in Isaiah 7:14 translated virgin (almah) can also be translated as "young woman." The idea is that Isaiah was simply saying that a "young woman" would give birth, not a virgin. While the near fulfillment of the Isaiah prophecy may have reference to a young woman giving birth, the far or ultimate fulfillment clearly points to a woman miraculously conceiving and giving birth. This is especially clear because the Old Testament never uses the word in a context other than virgin and because the Septuagint translates almah in Isaiah 7:14 categorically virgin (parthenos).

c. Immanuel: This title of Jesus refers to both His deity (God with us) and His identification and nearness to man (God with us).

i. Jesus is truly Immanuel, God with us. "Christ, indeed, was not called by this name Immanuel that we anywhere read of...but the import of this name is most truly affirmed and acknowledged to be fully made good in him." (Trapp, on Isaiah 7:14)

ii. "In what sense then, is Christ GOD WITH US? Jesus is called Immanuel, or God with us, in his incarnation; God with us, by the influences of his Holy Spirit, in the holy sacrament, in the preaching of his word, in private prayer. And God with us, through every action of our life, that we begin, continue, and end in his name. He is God with us, to comfort, enlighten, protect, and defend us, in every time of temptation and trial, in the hour of death, in the day of judgment; and God with us and in us, and we with and in him, to all eternity." (Clarke)

iii. We can deeply meditate on the meaning of this name – Immanuel.

It shows how low God bent down to save man; He added the nature of one of His own creatures to His own divine nature, accepting the weaknesses, frailties and dependency that the creature experiences.

It shows what a great miracle it was that God could add a human nature to His own and still remain God.

It shows the compatibility between the unfallen human nature and the divine nature; that the two could be joined shows that we are truly made in the image of God.

It shows that we can come to Him; if He has come to us, then we can come to Him. "Then, if Jesus Christ be 'God with us,' let us come to God without any question or hesitancy. Whoever you may be you need no priest or intercessor to introduce you to God, for God has introduced himself to you." (Spurgeon)

> iv. "John Wesley died with that upon his tongue, and let us live with it upon our hearts. – 'The best of all is God with us.'" (Spurgeon)

5. (24-25) Joseph marries Mary after the angelic announcement.

Then Joseph, being aroused from sleep, did as the angel of the Lord commanded him and took to him his wife, and did not know her till she had brought forth her firstborn Son. And he called His name JESUS.

Did as the angel of the Lord commanded: Joseph's obedience is notable. He did not doubt nor waver; he instantly understood the truth and the importance of the angelic messenger that came to him in the dream.

b. Did not know her till she had brought forth her firstborn Son: The words did not know her till imply that Joseph and Mary had normal marital relations after Jesus' birth.

> i. This emphasizes that Jesus was conceived miraculously. "Matthew wants to make Jesus' virginal conception quite unambiguous, for he adds that Joseph had no sexual union with Mary until she gave birth to Jesus." (Carson)

> ii. This also denies the Roman Catholic dogma of the perpetual virginity of Mary. "The marriage was thus formally completed, but not

consummated before the birth of Jesus. The Greek expression for not until would normally suggest that intercourse did take place after the end of this period…There is no biblical warrant for the tradition of the 'perpetual virginity' of Mary."

iii. This is an unbiblical doctrine which did not appear earlier than the fifth century after Jesus. It should be placed with the dogmas of Mary's Immaculate Conception, assumption into heaven, and present role as a mediator for believers. Each one of these is man's invention, meant to exalt Mary in an unbiblical manner.

c. And he called His name JESUS: They did what God told them to do. Though it was a fairly common name, it had a genuinely great meaning and would come to be the greatest name, the name above all names.

Genesis 1 – The Account of God's Creation

Genesis 1:1 – In the Beginning; Genesis 1:1-2 – Before the Beginning, At the Beginning; Genesis 1:3-23 – The First Five Days of Creation; Genesis 1:24-31 – The Sixth Day of Creation – The Creation of Man; A. Thoughts to begin with as we study the Bible.

1. We come to the Bible knowing there is a God.

a. There are many good and strong philosophical and logical reasons to believe in God. Yet the Bible does not make elaborate arguments for the existence of God. However, it does tell us how we can know God exists.

b. The Bible tells us we can know God exists because of what we see in the created world.

i. Psalm 19:1-4 explains this: The heavens declare the glory of God; and the firmament shows His handiwork. Day unto day utters speech, and night unto night reveals knowledge. There is no speech nor language where their voice is not heard. Their line has gone out through all the earth, and their words to the end of the world.

ii. Romans 1:20 also explains: For since the creation of the world His invisible attributes are clearly seen, being understood by the things that are made, even His eternal power and Godhead, so that they are without excuse.

c. This is an example of the teleological argument for the existence of God. It is the understanding that there must be a purposeful intelligence that created this world because the world shows both purpose and intelligence. In the view of many (including the author), this argument from purpose and design remains unanswered by the atheist or the agnostic.

2. We come to the Bible believing it is the place where God has spoken to man, perfectly and comprehensively.

a. We believe what is written in 2 Timothy 3:16-17: All Scripture is given by inspiration of God, and is profitable for doctrine, for reproof, for correction, for instruction in righteousness, that the man of God may be complete, thoroughly equipped for every good work.

i. We can study God, but we can't put Him under a microscope or test Him in a laboratory. We can only confidently know about Him what

He chooses to reveal to us. We are also confident that what He chooses to tell us is profitable and useful for us.

b. We believe the Bible must be understood literally, that is, as straightforward and true according to its literary context.

i. The Bible is much more than a book; it is a library of books, and books written in different literary forms. Some portions of the Bible give a historical account, others are poetic, and some are prophetic.

ii. We must understand the Bible literally according to its literary context. For example, when David wrote in Psalm 6:6: All night I make my bed swim; I drench my couch with my tears... he used a poetic literary form. We understand he didn't literally mean he cried so much that he flooded his room and set his bed afloat.

iii. Psalm 119:128 says: Therefore all Your precepts concerning all things I consider to be right. With great confidence, the Psalmist proclaimed the inerrancy of God's Word. It was right, not wrong; and it was right concerning all things.

When the Bible gives us history, it is right and true; the events actually happened as described.

When the Bible gives us poetry, it is right and true; the feeling and experiences were real for the writer and ring true to human experience.

When the Bible gives us prophecy, it is right and true; the events described will come to pass, just as it is written.

When the Bible gives us instruction, it is right and true; it truly does tell us the will of God and the best way of life.

When the Bible tells us of God, it is right and true; it reveals to us what the nature and heart and mind of God are, as much as we can comprehend.

iv. If we don't approach the Bible this way, then we can only come to it with how we feel about the text, and we decide what is true or false about the text – making ourselves greater than the text itself. Though the teachings of Scripture have many applications, they only have one true interpretation. Sometimes the interpretation is easy to discern and sometimes not, but God meant something with the text revealed to mankind.

v. "The only proper way to interpret Genesis 1 is not to 'interpret' it at all. That is, we accept the fact that it was meant to say exactly what it says." (Morris)

c. We believe the Bible is not a book of science; yet where it touches science, it speaks the truth. After all, if the Bible is false in regard to science or other things that we can prove, then we cannot regard it as reliable in regard to spiritual matters that we cannot objectively prove.

3. We come to the Bible knowing the copies we have in our hands are reliable duplicates (though not perfect duplicates) of the exact writings, which God perfectly inspired.

a. We can know this about the Old Testament by seeing the incredible care and reliability of the ancient Jewish scribes, demonstrated by the Dead Sea Scroll discoveries.

b . We can know this about the New Testament by knowing that because of earlier manuscripts, and a greater number of ancient manuscripts, the New Testament is by far the most reliable and exhaustively crosschecked ancient document we possess. Really, no more than one one-thousandth of the New Testament text is in question.

4. We come to the Bible knowing the unique importance of the Book of Genesis.

a. The Bible would be incomplete and perhaps incomprehensible without the Book of Genesis. It sets the stage for the entire drama of redemption, which unfolds in the rest of the book.

b. Almost all of the important doctrines and teachings of the Bible have their foundation in of Genesis.

    i. Genesis gives the foundation for the doctrines of:

Sin, the fall, redemption, justification.

The promise of the Messiah and Jesus Christ.

The personality and personhood of God.

The kingdom of God.

    ii. Genesis shows us the origin of:

The universe.

Order and complexity. The solar system.

The atmosphere and hydrosphere.

Life, man, marriage.

Good and evil.

Language, government, culture, nations, religion.

iii. It is precisely because people have abandoned the truth of Genesis that society is in such disarray.

c. Genesis is important to the New Testament. There are at least 165 passages in Genesis either directly quoted or clearly referred to in the New Testament; many of these are quoted more than once, so there are at least 200 quotations or allusions to Genesis in the New Testament.

i. In John 5:46-47, Jesus spoke of the importance of believing what Moses wrote: For if you believed Moses, you would believe Me; for he wrote about Me. But if you do not believe his writings, how will you believe My words? We can't truthfully and consistently say we believe in Jesus if we don't believe in the Book of Genesis.

ii. Martin Luther wrote: "I beg and faithfully warn every pious Christian not to stumble at the simplicity of the language and stories that will often meet him there [in Genesis]. He should not doubt that, however simple they may seem, these are the very words, works, judgments, and deeds of the high majesty, power, and wisdom of God" (cited in Boice).

5. According to the New Testament, Moses wrote the Book of Genesis (Luke 24:27 and 24:44). We can surmise that he did this with help from actual written records from the past God had preserved.

a. There are indicators of where these records begin and end. Note the phrasing of Genesis 2:4, 5:1, 6:9, 10:1, 11:10, 11:27, 25:12, 25:19, 36:1, 36:9, and 37:2.

b. In these passages phrases such as "this is the history" and "this is the book" and "this is the genealogy" may indicate the start or end of the records Moses collected.

i. "Thus it is probable that the Book of Genesis was written originally by actual eyewitnesses of the events reported therein. Probably the original narratives were recorded on tables of stone or clay, in common practice of early times, and then handed down from father to son, finally coming into the possession of Moses. Moses perhaps selected the appropriate sections for compilation, inserted his own editorial additions and comments, and provided smooth transitions from one document to the next, with the final result being the Book of Genesis as we have received it." (Morris)

B. The first five days of creation.

1. The philosophical importance of knowing God as creator.

a. The philosopher Jean-Paul Sartre and many others have stated the essential problem of philosophy: that there is something, instead of nothing. Why?

Everything else in our life flows from the answer to this question.

i. If everything around us, including ourselves, is the result of random, meaningless occurrences apart from the work of a creating God, then it says something about who I am, and where I, and the whole universe, are going. If that is the case then the only dignity or honor we bestow upon men is pure sentimentality, because we don't have any more significance than an amoeba and there is no greater law in the universe than survival of the fittest.

b. Some 100 years ago, there was a great German philosopher named Arthur Schopenhauer. By habit, he usually dressed like a vagrant, and one day he sat on a park bench in Berlin, deep in thought. His appearance made a policeman suspicious, so the policeman asked the philosopher "Who are you?" Schopenhauer answered, "I would to God I knew."

i. The only way we can ever really find out who we are is from God. The best place to find out begins in Genesis.

c. There are many possible answers to the question of how everything came into being. Some say, once there was absolutely nothing and now there is something. Others (including the Bible) say before there was anything created, there was a Personal Being.

d. There is a story saying that one day, students in a great physics professor's class – someone like Albert Einstein – said that they had decided there was no

God. The professor asked them how much of all the knowledge in the world they had among themselves collectively, as a class. The students discussed it for a while and decided they had 5% of all human knowledge among themselves. The professor thought their estimate was a little generous, but he asked them: "Is it possible God exists in the 95% you don't know?"

2. (1) A simple factual statement regarding God's work as Creator.

In the beginning God created the heavens and the earth.

a. God created: This summary statement will be detailed in the following verses, but the Bible simply and straightforwardly declares the world did not create itself or come about by chance. It was created by God who, by definition, is eternal and has always been.

i. "It is no accident that God is the subject of the first sentence of the Bible, for this word dominates the whole chapter and catches the eye at every point of the page: it is used some thirty-five times in as many verses of the story." (Kidner)

i.. If you believe Genesis 1:1, you really have no problem believing the rest of the Bible. The God big enough to have created the heavens and the earth is big enough to do all the rest the Bible says that He did and does.

b. God: This is the ancient Hebrew word Elohim. Grammatically it is a plural word used as if it were singular. The verbs and pronouns used with Elohim should be in the plural, but when Elohim refers to the LORD God the verbs and pronouns are in the singular.

i. Adam Clarke quoted Rabbi Simeon ben Joachi, commenting on the word Elohim: "Come and see the mystery of the word Elohim; there are three degrees, and each degree by itself alone, and yet notwithstanding they are all one, and joined together in one, and are not divided from each other." Clarke adds: "He must be strangely prejudiced indeed who cannot see that the doctrine of a Trinity, and of a Trinity in unity, is expressed in the above words."

ii. Luther on Elohim: "But we have clear testimony that Moses aimed to indicate the Trinity or the three persons in the one divine nature" (cited in Leupold).

c. God created the heavens: The simple fact of God's creation is even more amazing when we consider the greatness of God's universe.

i. A typical galaxy contains billions of individual stars; our galaxy alone (the Milky Way) contains 200 billion stars. Our galaxy is shaped like a giant spiral, rotating in space, with arms reaching out like a pinwheel, and our sun is one star on one arm of the pinwheel. It would take 250 million years for the pinwheel to make one full rotation. But this is only our galaxy; there are many other galaxies with many other shapes, including spirals, spherical clusters, and flat pancakes. The average distance between one galaxy and another is about 20 million trillion miles. Our closest galaxy is the

Andromeda Galaxy, about 12 million trillion miles away.

    ii. For every patch of sky the size of the moon, if you could look very deep, you would see about a million galaxies.

    iii. But God did all this Himself: Indeed My hand has laid the foundation of the earth, and My right hand has stretched out the heavens; when I call to them, they stand up together (Isaiah 48:13).

    iv. But God is bigger and greater than all His creation: Who has measured the waters in the hollow of His hand, measured heaven with a span and calculated the dust of the earth in a measure? (Isaiah 40:12).

God created the heavens anwwvwwwwwwvvd the earth: If God created the heavens and the earth, then we must forever put away the idea that anything happens by chance. "Chance" merely describes the statistical probability of something happening. Chance itself can neither do or perform anything.

    i. Some intelligent people may fall into this delusion. Jacques Monod, a biochemist, wrote: "Chance alone is at the source of every innovation, of all creation in the biosphere. Pure chance, absolutely free but blind, at the very root of the stupendous edifice of evolution."

    ii. But assigning such power to chance doesn't make sense. Chance has no power. For example, when a coin is flipped, the chance it will land heads is 50%; however, chance does not make it land heads. Whether or not it lands heads or tails is due to the strength with which the coin is flipped, the strength of air currents and air pressure as it flies through the air, where it is caught, and if it is flipped over once it is caught. Chance doesn't do anything but describe a probability.

ii. Many years ago a scientist named Carl Sagan petitioned the U.S. government for a grant to fund the search for intelligent life in outer space. He hoped to find evidence of life by using a super-sensitive instrument to pick up radio signals from distant space. When he received those radio signals, he looked for order and pattern, which demonstrated the signals were transmitted by intelligent life. In the same way, the order and pattern of the whole universe demonstrate that it was fashioned by intelligent life, not by chance. Scientists detect chance in the radio signals constantly (in the form of static with no pattern), but it tells them nothing.

iv. Therefore, when someone says the universe or anything else came about by chance, one may say that despite their expertise or skill in other areas, when it comes to this subject they are ignorant, superstitious, or simply repeating a tired theory said and disproved before, yet unthinkingly accepted.

e. God created: Inherent in the idea of God is that He is an intelligent designer. Only an intelligent designer could create a just-right universe, not chance. Our universe is a just-right universe. According to Hugh Ross in his book The Fingerprint of God:

    i. The universe has a just-right gravitational force. If it were larger, the stars would be too hot and would burn up too quickly and too unevenly to support life.

If it were smaller, the stars would remain so cool, nuclear fusion would never ignite, and there would be no heat and light.

    ii. The universe has a just-right speed of light.

If it were larger, stars would send out too much light.

If it were smaller, stars would not send out enough light.

    iii. The universe has a just-right average distance between the stars.

If it were larger, the heavy element density would be too thin for rocky planets to form, and there would only be gaseous planets.

If it were smaller, planetary orbits would become destabilized because of the gravitational pull from other stars.

    iv. The universe has a just-right polarity of the water molecule.

If it were greater, the heat of fusion and vaporization would be too great for life to exist.

If it were smaller, the heat of fusion and vaporization would be too small for life's existence, liquid water would become too inferior a solvent for life chemistry to proceed, ice would not float, leading to a runaway freeze-up.

v. We could conclude that there is no chance that such a universe could create itself, apart from an intelligent designer.

f. In the beginning God created the heavens and the earth: This tells us that God used no pre-existing material to create the earth. The ancient Hebrew word bara (created) is specific. It means to create out of nothing, showing that God created the world out of nothing, not out of Himself. God is separate from His creation. Unlike Eastern and pantheistic perceptions of God, the Bible teaches the universe could perish yet He would remain.

i. Men cannot create in the sense the term is used in Genesis 1:1. We can only fashion or form things out of existing material. The closest we come to creating is in reproducing ourselves sexually. This is perhaps one reason why Satan wants to pervert and destroy God's plan and standard for sexuality; it is deeply connected to our being made in the image of God.

ii. Louis Ginzberg relayed a fascinating legend on how the 22 letters of the Hebrew alphabet all wanted to begin the Bible, but in the end, the letter "bet" was allowed, because he said, "O Lord of the world! May it be Thy will to create Thy world through me, seeing that all the dwellers of the world give praise daily unto Thee through me, as it is said, Blessed be the Lord forever. Amen, and Amen." For this reason (according to the legend), the Hebrew Book of Genesis begins, "Bereshit God created the heaven and the earth."

3. The Bible's clear teaching of God's creation and the uncertainty of modern science.

a. Some scientists often act certain in their knowledge about the origin of the universe, but their continually revolutionary discoveries prove they are, in some way, feeling their way along in the dark. Honest scientists, those who resist pride or arrogance, appreciate how little they do know, and hold their present discoveries with a sense of humility.

b. Some scientists may be overly sure when it comes to what can be known of the universe, but we do not have to accept such arrogance. The constantly changing scene of science is illustrated by a sidebar to a science article many years ago in the Los Angeles Times titled, "The Big Bang and What Followed It":

In the beginning, there was light – but also quarks and electrons. The Big Bang spewed out energy that condensed into radiation and particles. The quarks joined into protons and careened wildly about in a hot, dense, glowing goop as opaque as a star.

Time (300,000 years or so) passed. Space expanded. Matter cooled. The electrons and protons, electrically irresistible to each other, merged into neutral hydrogen, and from this marriage, the first atoms were born.

Space between atoms became as transparent as crystal – pretty much the way it looks today.

The rest, as they say, is history. Atoms merged to form dust clouds, which grew into stars and galaxies and clusters. Stars used up their nuclear fuel, collapsed and exploded in recurring cycles, fusing elements in the process.

Occasionally, a stable planet condensed around a second-generation star, where carbon-based life forms grew into, among other things, cosmologists, the better to contemplate it all.

c. In 1913, an astronomer in Arizona discovered that stars appeared to be moving away from the earth at tremendous speeds, up to two million miles an hour. In 1919, another American astronomer named Edwin Hubble used this information to develop a theory of an expanding universe, which is the foundation of the "Big Bang" idea. Early on, other scientists discovered background radiation from all parts of the universe, which they suppose is the leftover "noise" from the first great explosion. But scientists are really not much closer at all to knowing anything about this instant beginning to the universe.

d. In fact, the more they find out, the more they discover how much they don't know. There was a time when astrophysicists were faced with another challenge: trying to figure out what "dark matter" is. Dark matter is a term some scientists use to explain an enormous apparent excess of gravity in the universe. Dark matter may make up 99.9% of everything in the universe, but no one knows what it is.

Though suggestions are offered, they are only suggestions. David O. Caldwell of the University of California at Santa Barbara said, "When it comes to dark matter, the only thing that we are convinced of at the moment is that it's there." But actually, scientists cannot even agree on that! Michael S. Turner, an astrophysics professor at the University of Chicago, said: "It's very humbling. The origin, composition, energy and mass of the most common matter in the entire universe is unknown."

e. This uncertainty is shown in a March 6, 1995, front-page article in the Los Angeles Times headlined, "Rethinking Cosmic Questions":

Ever since people first stood up amid the tall grasses and looked about the world in wonder, religion, mythology and science all have struggled to explain how the world came to be. But when it comes to creation stories, few can hold a candle to the tale cooked up by modern cosmologists.

Dialing back the cosmic clock about 15 billion years, they depict a time before time, a place before space existed. Out of nothing and nowhere, all the energy and matter in the universe exploded into existence in an event that came to be called… the Big Bang.

While masterfully spinning ideas out of faith and equations, cosmologists were pitifully short on data. They could not see or measure the phenomena they were trying to explain. "Twenty-five years ago, cosmology was very close to religion," said physicist Roberto Peccei of UCLA.

Experimental cosmologist Chris Stubbs of the University of Washington, "You've got these things that are ridiculously far away and ridiculously faint, and… you've got to make sense out of it."

"At times, I miss the old days when I could just work in my office and not worry that someone would disprove my theory in a few weeks," said Rocky Kold of the Fermi National Accelerator Laboratory in Illinois.

"Many of us who have worked in this field for decades still worry that the whole house of cards is going to collapse," said Princeton cosmologist David Wilkinson.

Recent observations, for example, suggest that the universe is younger than its oldest stars – an enigma that has astronomers scrambling for explanations.

The biggest mystery, however, strikes even scientists as so astonishing as to be absurd: 99% of the universe, according to some estimates, is made of totally unfamiliar stuff. Commonly known as dark matter, it is actually mostly transparent; it neither shines nor casts a shadow. Whatever it is, it is not like us… According to some theories, it also is the glue that holds the universe together, and keeps it from expanding forever into endless space.

f. "The study of human origins seems to be a field in which each discovery raises the debate to a more sophisticated level of uncertainty." (Christopher Stringer of the Natural Museum of London)

4. One may doubt the ability of many modern scientists to answer the question of origins. But that does not automatically give us confidence in the answer found in the Book of Genesis. Some believe that Genesis only records a creation myth, meant only to show the greatness of God in poetic grandeur. Though there are poetic elements to the account, we believe it was still written to record a historical reality. Other Scriptures, in their approach to Genesis 1, demonstrate this.

a. Psalm 136 connects the Genesis account of creation with the rest of Israel's history in a seamless fabric. The creation account is not put in a category of historical fiction.

b. Jesus quoted Genesis as if it were a purely historical record (Matthew 19:4-6 and 23:35).

c. C.S. Lewis wrote that when he heard a Biblical scholar claim the Genesis creation account was a myth, he didn't want to know about the man's credentials as a Biblical scholar. He wanted to know how many myths the man had read. Myths were Lewis' business as a literary scholar, and he could see the Biblical account of creation was unlike mythical accounts.

d. It is true that Genesis was not written primarily as a scientific document. But if God gave us a truly scientific, detailed account of creation, written in scientific language, there would be no one who could understand it and no end to the length of such an account. Even if it were written in simple, 20th-century scientific language, it would have made no sense to all previous generations and no sense to future generations either.

e. It is the glory of God to conceal a matter, but the glory of kings is to search out a matter (Proverbs 25:2). Scientific inquiry is the glory of man; yet it must all be done with utmost humility, realizing God conceals these matters for man to search out.

5. God did all this in the beginning, yet there was much before the beginning.

a. In the beginning, God: God Himself was before the beginning: Your throne is established from of old; You are from everlasting (Psalm 93:2). Some are troubled by the questions, "Where did God come from?" and "Who created God?" The answer is found in the definition of God – that God is the uncreated Being, eternal – without beginning or end.

i. This is demonstrated in several passages of Scripture. LORD, You have been our dwelling place in all generations. Before the mountains were brought forth, or ever You had formed the earth and the world, even from everlasting to everlasting, You are God (Psalm 90:1-2).

ii. J. Edwin Orr used a memorable definition of God, which was thoroughly Biblical: God is the only infinite, eternal, and unchangeable spirit, the perfect being in whom all things begin, and continue, and end.

b. In the beginning, God: God was in three Persons before the beginning, and the Persons shared a relationship of love and fellowship: "O Father, glorify Me together with Yourself, with the glory which I had with You before the world was…for You loved Me before the foundation of the world" (John 17:5, 17:24).

c. In the beginning, God: Before the beginning, there was an eternal purpose in the heart of God (Ephesians 3:11) to gather together in one all things in Christ (Ephesians 1:10). God's purpose was to "resolve" or "sum up" all things in Jesus as if Jesus Himself were the answer to a great and complex problem God wrote out on the "blackboard" of the universe.

d. In the beginning, God: Before the beginning, God had a specific plan to fulfill this eternal purpose, with many different aspects revealed to us:

i. The mission of Jesus was foreordained before the foundation of the world: He indeed was foreordained before the foundation of the world, but was manifest in these last times for you (1 Peter 1:20).

ii. Eternal life was promised before time began: in hope of eternal life which God, who cannot lie, promised before time began (Titus 1:2).

iii. The mystery of the gospel (the cross) was foreordained before the ages: But we speak the wisdom of God in a mystery, the hidden wisdom which God ordained before the ages for our glory (1 Corinthians 2:7).

iv. The grace given unto us was given before the world began: who has saved us and called us with a holy calling, not according to our works, but according to His own purpose and grace which was given to us in Christ Jesus before time began (2 Timothy 1:9).

v. Believers in Jesus Christ were chosen in Him before the foundation of the world: just as He chose us in Him before the foundation of the world, that we should be holy and without blame before Him in love (Ephesians 1:4).

e. In the beginning, God: At some time before the beginning, God created the angels, because they witnessed the creation of the heavens and the earth (Job 38:7).

6. (2) The state of the earth before God organized creation.

The earth was without form, and void; and darkness was on the face of the deep. And the Spirit of God was hovering over the face of the waters.

a. The earth was without form, and void: Some translate the idea in this verse as the earth became without form and void. Their thinking is the earth was originally created not without form and void, but it became without form and void through the destructive work of Satan. However, this is not the plain grammatical sense of the ancient Hebrew.

i. Those who follow this idea look to Isaiah 45:18: For thus says the LORD, Who created the heavens, Who is God, Who formed the earth and made it, Who has established it, Who did not create it in vain, Who formed it to be inhabited: "I am the LORD, and there is no other." The idea, here, is God says He did not create the world in vain (the Hebrew word is the same as the word for void in Genesis 1:1).

ii. Based on these ideas, some have advanced what has been called the "Gap Theory." It is the idea that there was a long and indefinite chronological gap between Genesis 1:1 and 1:2. Most gap theory advocates use the theory to explain the fossil record, assigning old and extinct fossils to this indefinite gap.

iii. Whatever merit the gap theory may have, it cannot explain the extinction and fossilization of ancient animals. The Bible says plainly death came by Adam (Romans 5:12), and since fossils are the result of death, they could not have happened before Adam's time.

b. Darkness was on the face of the deep: This may describe a sense of resistance to the moving of the Holy Spirit on the earth. Some speculate this was because Satan was cast down to the earth (Isaiah 14:12; Ezekiel 28:16) and resisted God's plan, though his resistance was futile.

c. The Spirit of God was hovering over the face of the waters: When God began to transform the earth into something beautiful and compatible with His great plan, He started with the work of the Spirit of God. The Holy Spirit begins every work of creation or re-creation.

i. "The first divine act in fitting up this planet for the habitation of man was for the Spirit of God to move upon the face of the waters. Till that time, all was formless, empty, out of order, and in confusion. In a word, it was chaos; and to make it into that thing of beauty which the world is at the present moment, even though it is a fallen world, it was needful that the movement of the Spirit of God should take place upon it." (Spurgeon)

ii. Leupold on the Spirit of God was hovering: "The verb… signifies a vibrant moving, a protective hovering… His was the preparatory work for leading over from the inorganic to the organic."

iii. Hovering: "Any impression of Olympian detachment which the rest of the chapter might have conveyed is forestalled by the simile of the motherbird 'hovering' (Moffatt) or fluttering by her brood. The verb reappears in Deuteronomy 32:11 to describe the eagle's movements in stirring its young into flight." (Kidner)

d. **The earth was without form, and void:** When God created the earth, He quite likely built an "old" earth, creating things in the midst of a time sequence, with either apparent or manufactured age built into creation.

i. For example, Adam was already of mature age when he was created; there was age purposefully built in. Likewise, the trees in the Garden of Eden had rings in them, and there were undoubtedly canyons and sandy beaches in Adam's world.

2. (3-5) The first day of creation: light is created and divided from the darkness.

Then God said, "Let there be light"; and there was light. And God saw the light, that it was good; and God divided the light from the darkness. God called the light Day, and the darkness He called Night. So the evening and the morning were the first day.

a. Let there be light: The first step from chaos to order is to bring light. This is also the way God works in our life.

i. Paul wrote about the light brought to us by the gospel: But even if our gospel is veiled, it is veiled to those who are perishing, whose minds the god of this age has blinded, who do not believe, lest the light of the gospel of the glory of Christ, who is the image of God, should shine on them. For we do not preach ourselves, but Christ Jesus the Lord, and ourselves your bondservants for Jesus' sake. For it is the God who commanded light to shine out of darkness, who has shone in our hearts to give the light of the knowledge of the glory of God in the face of Jesus Christ (2 Corinthians 4:3-6).

b. Then God said: God did not have to fashion light with His hands. It was enough for God to merely speak the words, Light be! And there was light.

i. "I must have you notice that this light came instantaneously. The Hebrew suggests this far better than our translation–it is sublimely brief. 'Light be: light was.'" (Spurgeon)

ii. Because God created things by speaking them into existence, some have said we can operate on the same principle, speaking things into existence by faith. This is often based on a wrong understanding of Hebrews 11:3 (by faith we understand that the worlds were framed by the word of God), which is taken to say, God Himself used faith in creating the world. Instead, it says it is by faith we understand God created the world.

iii. Also, some have a wrong understanding of Mark 11:22 which is taken to literally mean "have God's faith" as if we are to have the same faith God has. But the words Jesus answered and said to them, "Have faith in God" cannot mean this, because faith, as Hebrews 11:1 tells us, is the substance of things hoped for, the evidence of things not seen. What does God hope for? What does He not see? An omnipotent, omniscient Being certainly does not need faith. He is the object of faith as well as the source of faith (Ephesians 2:8).

c. There was light: Genesis tells us that light, day, and night each existed before the sun and the moon were created on the fourth day (Genesis 1:14-19). This shows us that light is more than a physical substance; it also has a supernatural aspect. In the new heavens and the new earth, there won't be any sun or moon. God Himself will be the light (Revelation 22:5).

i. The darkness God later sent upon the Egyptians (Exodus 10:21) had a tangible quality to it, far beyond what we usually think of as being associated with darkness; it could be felt. This demonstrates a certain supernatural element, which can be related to light and darkness.

d. So the evening and the morning were the first day: Many wonder if this was a literal day (in the sense we think of a day) or if it was a geological age. Some say that God created the world in six days, and others say He created it in six vast geological ages. Though there is disagreement among Christians on this, the plainest and simplest meaning of the text is that He created in six days as we think of days.

i. "If the days were not days at all, would God have countenanced the word? Does He trade in inaccuracies, however edifying? The question hinges on the proper use of language." (Kidner)

ii. "There ought to be no need of refuting the idea that yom means period. Reputable dictionaries… know nothing of this notion. Hebrew dictionaries are our primary source of reliable information concerning Hebrew words." (Leupold)

iii. "This is, no doubt, a literal and accurate account of God's first day's work in the creation of the world." (Spurgeon)

8. (6-8) The second day of creation: God makes an atmospheric division.

Then God said, "Let there be a firmament in the midst of the waters, and let it divide the waters from the waters." Thus God made the firmament, and divided the waters which were under the firmament from the waters which were above the firmament; and it was so. And God called the firmament Heaven. So the evening and the morning were the second day.

a. Let there be a firmament: The idea of a firmament is of an expanse (NIV, NAS) or space (NLT). The waters of the land are separated from the water vapor in the sky.

b. The waters which were above the firmament: Some commentators and scientists believe that here the Bible recognizes the existence of significant water vapor in the sky. Such a vapor blanket would greatly change the ecology of the earth, and Henry Morris suggests several effects of a vapor blanket:

i. "The waters above the firmament thus probably constituted a vast blanket of water vapor above the troposphere and possibly above the stratosphere as well, in the high temperature region now known as the ionosphere, and extending far into space." (Morris)

ii. It would serve as a global greenhouse, maintaining an essentially uniform, pleasant temperature all over the world.

iii. Without great temperature variations, there would be no significant winds, and the water-rain cycle could not form. There would be no rain, as we know it today.

iv. There would be lush, tropical-like vegetation all over the world, fed not by rain, but by a rich evaporation and condensation cycle, resulting in heavy dew or ground-fog.

v. The vapor blanket would filter out ultraviolet radiation, cosmic rays, and other destructive energies bombarding the planet. These are known to be the cause of mutations, which decrease human longevity. Human and animal lifespans would be greatly increased.

vi. A vapor blanket would provide the necessary reservoir for a potential worldwide flood.

9. (9-13) The third day of creation: the land is divided from the sea; plants and all types of vegetation are created.

Then God said, "Let the waters under the heavens be gathered together into one place, and let the dry land appear"; and it was so. And God called the dry land Earth, and the gathering together of the waters He called Seas. And God saw that it was good. Then God said, "Let the earth bring forth grass, the herb that yields seed, and the fruit tree that yields fruit according to its kind, whose seed is in itself, on the earth"; and it was so. And the earth brought forth grass, the herb that yields seed according to its kind, and the tree that yields fruit, whose seed is in itself according to its kind. And God saw that it was good. So the evening and the morning were the third day.

a. Let the waters under the heavens be gathered together: The idea is that before this, the earth was covered with water. Now the waters are gathered together into one place, and dry land appears.

b. Let the earth bring forth grass: All this happened before the creation of the Sun (the fourth day of creation, Genesis 1:14-19). This means the plants must have had sufficient nourishment because of the light God had created before the sun and the moon (in Genesis 1:3).

i. Those who propose these days of creation were not literal days, but successive ages of slow, evolutionary development have a real problem here. It is hard to explain how plants and all vegetation could grow and thrive eons before the sun and the moon. No modern evolutionist would argue plant life is older than the sun or the moon, but this is what the Genesis record tells us.

ii. Many wonder how the sun, moon, and stars were created on the fourth day when light (including day and night) was created on the first day. Many have suggested the problem is solved by saying these heavenly bodies were created on the first day, but were not specifically visible, or not finally formed, until the fourth. But Revelation tells us of a coming day when we won't need the sun, moon, and stars any longer (Revelation 21:23). There's no reason why God couldn't have started creation in the same way He will end it.

b. And it was so: This is the beginning of life on planet earth, directly created by God, not slowly evolving over millions of years.

i. Some scientists now say life on earth began when immense meteorites carrying amino acids impacted earth at a time when the sun was cooler and the earth was a watery ball covered with ice up to 1,000 feet thick. The idea is that a meteor hit the ice, broke through, and "seeded" the water underneath with the building blocks of life, which assembled into an "organic soup." However the process was triggered, the scientists said life on earth began in "a geological instant." But by an instant, they mean 10 million years or less. In the opinion of the author, it takes more faith to believe this than to believe in Genesis.

ii. The fossil evidence is more consistent with the idea that life exploded into existence on earth, instead of slowly evolving.

c. The earth brought forth grass, the herb that yields seed… and the tree that yields fruit, whose seed is in itself: The plants were created not as seeds, but as full-grown plants each bearing seeds. They were thus created as mature plants, having the appearance of age. The chicken really did come before the egg.

d. According to its kind: This phrase appears ten times in Genesis chapter 1. It means God allows variation within a kind, but something of one kind will never develop into something of another kind.

e. And God saw that it was good: God knows what is good. He is not some vague moral neutral. He knows what is good and organizes His creation to result in something good.

i. God does not call the earth good until it has become habitable, a place where man can live.

f. Let the earth bring forth… every herb that yields seed… the herb that yields seed according to its kind… And God saw that it was good: Some use this passage to justify the use of drugs (especially marijuana) because grass and every herb came forth at God's command. But certainly, not every herb is good for every purpose. Hemlock is natural, but not good.

i. In fact, the use of drugs in this manner is nowhere approved and is always condemned in the Bible. The wrong use of drugs is often associated with sorcery and the occult.

ii. Sorcery is universally condemned in the Bible (Exodus 22:18, Deuteronomy 18:10, 2 Chronicles 33:6, Revelation 21:8 and 22:15). In both the Old and New Testaments, the word sorcery was connected with the making and taking of drugs.

10. (14-19) The fourth day of creation: the sun, moon, and stars.

Then God said, "Let there be lights in the firmament of the heavens to divide the day from the night; and let them be for signs and seasons, and for days and years; and let them be for lights in the firmament of the heavens to give light on the earth"; and it was so. Then God made two great lights: the greater light to rule the day, and the lesser light to rule the night. He made the stars also. God set them in the firmament of the heavens to give light on the earth, and to rule over the day and over the night, and to divide the light from the darkness. And God saw that it was good. So the evening and the morning were the fourth day.

a. Let them be for signs and seasons: God made the sun and the moon – these lights in the firmament of the heavens to be for signs and seasons. Since the beginning, man has used God's provision of the sun, moon, and stars to mark and measure time and direction.

b. God set them in the firmament of the heavens: God knew exactly how far to set the sun from the earth. A few million miles more or less and life as we know it would be impossible.

i. The intricate balance of our ecosystem argues strongly for the existence of a Creator. We live in a very complex world.

ii. Ginzberg quotes a Jewish legend connecting the movement of the sun to the praise of God (as in Psalms 113:3, 50:1, and 148:3): "The progress of the sun in his circuit is an uninterrupted song of praise to God. And this song alone makes his motion possible. Therefore, when Joshua wanted to bid the sun stand still, he had to command him to be silent. His song of praise hushed, the sun stood still."

c. Let them be for signs and seasons: When God set the lights in the heavens to be for signs, it probably includes what we commonly call the constellations, but was called by the ancient Hebrews the Mazzaroth (Job 38:31-32).

i. Significantly, the sequence of the zodiac is the same in every language and culture, even if the specific names of the constellations change. Also, we know the figures of the constellations suggested to us don't look like those things at all, and, they never did. Yet the names for the figures of the constellations are the same in all cultures. This points to a common, pre-Babel beginning for all these things before the truth of the constellations was corrupted.

ii. Luke 1:70 and Acts 3:21 speak of holy prophets since the world began. These prophets may be the stars themselves. Psalm 147:4 and Isaiah 40:26 tell us God has the stars all numbered and God has a name for them all. Psalm 6-19:1 tells us the heavens contain a message from God.

iii. Astrology is a satanic corruption of God's original message in the stars, a message outlining His plan of redemption. Because astrology is a corruption, it is to be avoided always by man (Isaiah 47:12-15).

d. He made the stars also: With all the other stars in our universe, we often wonder if there is life on other planets.

i. When you take into account all that is necessary for the sustenance of life, as we know it, there are few planets able to support life. Taking into account factors such as our galaxy type, star location, star age, star mass, star color, distance from stars, axis tilt, rotation period, surface gravity, tidal force, magnetic field, oxygen quantity in atmosphere, atmospheric pressure, and 20 other important factors, the probability of all 33 occurrences happening on any one planet is one in 10 to the 42nd power. The total number of possible planets in the universe is 10 to the 22nd power.

ii. At one time the U.S. government spent $100 million a year looking for extraterrestrial intelligence. It might have been wiser to spend the money cultivating intelligent life in Washington or other centers of government.

11. (20-23) The fifth day of creation: birds and sea creatures are created.

Then God said, "Let the waters abound with an abundance of living creatures, and let birds fly above the earth across the face of the firmament of the heavens." So God created great sea creatures and every living thing that moves, with which the waters abounded, according to their kind, and every winged bird according to its kind. And God saw that it was good. And God blessed them, saying, "Be fruitful and multiply, and fill the waters in the seas, and let birds multiply on the earth." So the evening and the morning were the fifth day.

a. Let the waters abound with an abundance of living creatures: We see the great variety of birds and sea creatures were created at the same time, not evolving slowly over millions of years. Even though plant life was created before animal life, animal life was not created out of plant life.

i. Among the diversity of animals, many share similar structures: birds, reptiles, mammals, and so forth. This argues at least as persuasively for a common Designer as it does for a common life source. All life did not come from the same primordial cell, but it did all come from the same Designer.

b. According to their kind: Again, all animal life is created according to its kind. God deliberately structured plenty of variation within a kind, but one "kind" does not become another.

i. For example, structure among dogs is diverse. The teacup poodle is very different from the Great Dane, but they are both dogs. However, they won't become mice, no matter how much breeding is done.

ii. Evolutionists often give convincing examples of microevolution, the variation of a kind within its kind, adapting to the environment. For example, the ratio of black to white peppered moths may increase when pollution makes it easier for dark moths to escape detection; or finches may develop different beaks in response to their distinctive environment. But the moths are still moths, and the finches are still finches. There has been no change outside of the kind. Microevolution does not prove macroevolution.

12. Doesn't the fossil record show these creatures slowly evolved into existence, instead of suddenly appearing?

a. Most people are unaware that Darwin's strongest opponents were not clergymen, but fossil experts. Darwin admitted the state of the fossil evidence was "the most obvious and gravest objection which can be urged against my theory," and because of the fossil evidence, "all the most eminent paleontologists… and all our greatest geologists… have unanimously, often vehemently, maintained" that the species do not change.

b. The fossil record is marked by two great principles: first, stasis, which means most species are unchanged in all their documented history. The way they look when they first appear in the fossil record is the way they look when last appearing in the fossil record. They have not changed. Second, sudden appearance, which means in any local area, a species does not arise gradually, but appears all at once and "fully formed."

  i. Philip Johnson: "If evolution means the gradual change of one kind of organism into another kind, the outstanding characteristic of the fossil record is the absence of evidence for evolution."

c. The Bighorn Basin in Wyoming contains a continuous record of fossil deposits for what geologists say is five million years. Because this record is so complete, paleontologists assumed a positive trail of evolution could be found. Instead, "the fossil record does not convincingly document a single transition from one species to another" (Johnson).

  i. Evolutionist Nile Eldredge wrote: "We paleontologists have said that the history of life [in the fossil record] supports [the story of gradual evolution], all the while knowing that it does not" (Johnson).

d. Either evolution happened slowly, with each tiny change building on the last, over billions of years; or the changes came as quick leaps: something like a mouse coming out of a snake's egg.

i. The fossil record totally rejects the idea of millions of tiny changes; the quick leaps are a way of attributing miraculous power to "chance" or "nature" instead of God. While admiring the faith of those who believe in such hopeful monsters, it seems far more rational to believe in a wise, creating, designing God.

C. The sixth day of creation: the creation of man.

1. (24-25) God makes land animals.

Then God said, "Let the earth bring forth the living creature according to its kind: cattle and creeping thing and beast of the earth, each according to its kind"; and it was so. And God made the beast of the earth according to its kind, cattle according to its kind, and everything that creeps on the earth according to its kind. And God saw that it was good.

a. Let the earth bring forth the living creature: On the fifth day of creation, God made birds and sea animals, but now God turned His creative attention towards land animals of various types.

b. God made the beast of the earth according to its kind: When we look at the infinite variety of the animal kingdom (both living and extinct), we must be impressed with God's creative power, as well as His sense of humor. Any Being who makes the giraffe, the platypus, and the peacock is a God of joy and humor.

> i. To a peahen, the most attractive peacocks are the ones with the biggest fans, but the big fan on the tail makes it difficult to escape a predator. Therefore, the peahen rewards the peacock with the least chance of survival. This is one example of a natural phenomenon that presents a great problem for the idea of survival of the fittest.

c. According to its kind: Again, this important phrase is emphasized. God allows tremendous variation within a kind, but one kind will never become another kind.

2. (26) God plans to make man in His image.

Then God said, "Let Us make man in Our image, according to Our likeness; let them have dominion over the fish of the sea, over the birds of the air, and over the cattle, over all the earth and over every creeping thing that creeps on the earth."

a. Let Us make man in Our image: The repeated use of the plural (Let Us… in Our image, according to Our likeness) is consistent with the idea that there is One God in three Persons, what we know as the Trinity.

> i. Leupold does a good job showing that the plurality of let Us make cannot be merely the plurality of royalty, nor can it be God speaking with and to the angels. It is an indicator of the Trinity, though not clearly spelled out.

b. In Our image: An understanding of who man is begins with knowing we are made in the image of God. Man is different from every other order of created being because He has a created consistency with God.

i. This means there is an unbridgeable gap between human life and animal life. Though we are biologically similar to certain animals, we are distinct in our moral, intellectual, and spiritual capabilities.

ii. This means there is also an unbridgeable gap between human life and angelic life. Nowhere are we told the angels are made in the image of God. Angels cannot have the same kind of relationship of love and fellowship with God we can have.

iii. This means the incarnation was truly possible. God (in the second Person of the Trinity) could really become man because although deity and humanity are not the same, they are compatible.

iv. This means human life has intrinsic value, quite apart from the "quality of life" experienced by any individual, because human life is made in the image of God.

c. In Our image: There are several specific things in man that show him to be made in the image of God.

Mankind alone has a natural countenance looking upward.

Mankind alone has such a variety of facial expressions.

Mankind alone has a sense of shame expressing itself in a blush.

Mankind alone speaks.

Mankind alone possesses personality, morality, and spirituality.

In Our image: There are at least three aspects to the idea that we are made in the image of God.

It means humans possess personality: knowledge, feelings, and a will. This sets man apart from all animals and plants.

It means humans possess morality: we are able to make moral judgments and have a conscience.

It means humans possess spirituality: man is made for communion with God. It is on the level of spirit we communicate with God.

e. In Our image: This does not mean that God has a physical or human body. God is Spirit (John 4:24). Though God does not have a physical body, He designed man so his physical body could do many of the things God does: see, hear, smell, touch, speak, think, plan, and so forth.

i. "It will hardly be safe to say that the body of man is patterned after God, because God, being an incorporeal spirit, cannot have what we term a material body. Yet the body of man must at least be regarded as the fittest receptacle for the man's spirit and so must bear at least an analogy that is so close that God and His angels choose to appear in human form when they appear to men." (Leupold)

f. In Our image, according to Our likeness: The terms for image and likeness are slightly different. Image has more to do with appearance, and likeness has more to do with an abstract similarity, but they both essentially mean the same thing here in this context.

g. Let them have dominion: Before God ever created man, He decreed that man would have dominion over the earth. Man's pre-eminence of the created order and his ability to affect his environment is no accident; it is part of God's plan for man and the earth.

i. In this sense, it is sin if man does not use this dominion responsibly, in the sense of a proper regard for stewardship on this earth.

3. (27-31) God's creation of man and initial commission to Adam.

So God created man in His own image; in the image of God He created him; male and female He created them. Then God blessed them, and God said to them, "Be fruitful and multiply; fill the earth and subdue it; have dominion over the fish of the sea, over the birds of the air, and over every living thing that moves on the earth." And God said, "See, I have given you every herb that yields seed which is on the face of all the earth, and every tree whose fruit yields seed; to you it shall be for food. Also, to every beast of the earth, to every bird of the air, and to everything that creeps on the earth, in which there is life, I have given every green herb for food"; and it was so. Then God saw everything that He had made, and indeed it was very good. So the evening and the morning were the sixth day.

a. So God created man in His own image: God created man according to His plan as described in Genesis 1:26. The concept of man being created in the image of God is repeated to give emphasis to the idea.

i. We are plainly told God created man fully formed, and created him in one day, not gradually over millions of years of progressive evolution. The idea that a slow, progressive evolution could produce a complex mechanism like the human body just doesn't hold up.

ii. It is said there would be at least 40 different stages of evolution required to form an eye. What possible benefit could there be for the first 39 stages? The mathematician D.S. Ulam argues it was highly improbable for the eye to evolve by the accumulation of small mutations because the number of mutations must be so large and the time available was not nearly long enough for them to appear. Evolutionist Ernst Mayr commented: "Somehow or other by adjusting these figures we will come out all right. We are comforted by the fact that evolution has occurred." Johnson observes: "Darwinism to them was not a theory open to refutation but a fact to be accounted for" (Johnson).

iii. Darwin wrote: "If it could be demonstrated that any complex organ existed which could not possibly have been formed by numerous, successive, slight modifications, my theory would absolutely break down." Professor Richard Goldschmidt, a geneticist at the University of California at Berkley, listed a series of complex structures (from the hair of mammals to hemoglobin) he thought could not have been produced by thousands of years of small mutations. "The Darwinists met this fantastic suggestion with savage ridicule. As Goldschmidt put it, 'This time I was not only crazy but almost a criminal'... To suppose that such a random event could reconstruct even a single complex organ like a liver or kidney is about as reasonable as to suppose that an improved watch can be designed by throwing an old one against the wall" (Johnson).

b. **Male and female He created them:** This should not be construed to mean Adam was originally some type of androgynous being, being both male and female. This passage of Genesis gives us an overview of God's creation of man, and Genesis 2 will explain how exactly God created male and female.

i. In our day, many say there is no real difference between men and women. This makes sense if we are the result of mindless evolution, but not if it is true that **male and female He created them.** To God, the differences between men and women are not accidents. Since He created them, the differences are good and meaningful.

ii. Men are not women, and women are not men. One of the saddest signs of our culture's depravity is the amount and the degree of gender confusion today.

iii. It is vain to wonder if men or women are superior to the other. A man is absolutely superior at being a man. A woman is absolutely superior at being a woman. But when a man tries to be a woman or a woman tries to be a man, you have something inferior.

c. Then God blessed them: the first thing God did for man was to bless him. Without the goodness of God's blessing, human life would be not only unbearable but also impossible.

d. Be fruitful and multiply; fill the earth and subdue it; have dominion: God also gives man a job to do: fulfill God's intention of man's exercise of dominion over the earth. Inherent in this command is that man should be fruitful and multiply and fill the earth. Man cannot fulfill God's plan for him on the earth unless he populates it.

i. Additionally, God gave mankind a desire for sex, which would make the populating of the earth quick and likely.

ii. However, many have thought that being fruitful and multiplying was God's only or main purpose for sex, but this isn't the case. The primary reason God created sex was to contribute to the bonding of a oneflesh relationship.

iii. Animals have sexual relations only for reproduction, but human sexual response is different from animal sexual response in many ways. Human ovulation has no outward sign; humans have sex in private; humans have secondary sexual characteristics (only in humans do females develop breasts before the first birth). Only humans demonstrate a constant availability for and interest in sex, as opposed to a "heat" season in animals. In humans, the duration of the sexual interlude is longer and the intensity of the pleasure of sex is stronger, and only humans continue to have intercourse after the end of fertility. None of these specifically human dimensions of sex are required for reproduction, but all of them are useful for sex as a tool of bonding.

e. To you it shall be for food: God gave man dominion over the whole earth, but only vegetation is specifically mentioned as being for food. Seemingly, before the flood, the human race was vegetarian, but after the flood, man was given permission to eat the flesh of animals (Genesis 9:3).

f. God saw everything that He had made, and indeed it was very good: God's final analysis of His work of creation is that it was very good. God was pleased with His creation, and so are we!

i. When God pronounced the creation good, He really meant it. At the time, it was entirely good; there was no death or decay on earth at all.

4. The fossil discoveries of our so-called human ancestors such as Australopithecus afarensis, Australopithecus africanus, Homo habilis, and Homo

erectus show that the search for our human ancestors has been one filled with dishonest science and wishful thinking.

a. Quoting Johnson: "The psychological atmosphere that surrounds the viewing of hominid fossils is uncannily reminiscent of the veneration of relics at a medieval shrine." In 1984, the American Museum of Natural History held an unprecedented showing of original fossils said to depict human evolution titled Ancestors.

b. From Johnson: "The 'priceless and fragile relics' were carried by anxious curators in first-class airplane seats and brought to the Museum in a VIP motorcade of limousines with police escort. Inside the Museum, the relics were placed behind bullet-proof glass to be admired by a select preview audience of anthropologists, who spoke in hushed voices because 'It was like discussing theology in a cathedral.' A sociologist observing this ritual of the anthropologist tribe remarked, 'Sounds like ancestor worship to me.'"

c. Solly Zuckerman is a committed evolutionist and one of Britain's most influential scientists. He also regards much of the fossil evidence for human evolution as nonsense. Zuckerman has subjected key fossils to years of biometric testing and declares that the idea that they walked and ran upright is flimsy wishful thinking. He remarked that the record of reckless speculation in the field of human origins "is so astonishing that it is legitimate to ask whether much science is yet to be found in this field at all" .

d. "The story of human descent from apes is not merely a scientific hypothesis; it is the secular equivalent of the story of Adam and Eve, and a matter of immense cultural importance. Propagating the story requires illustrations, museum exhibits, and television reenactments. It also requires a priesthood, in the form of thousands of researchers, teachers, and artists who provide realistic and imaginative detail and carry the story out to the general public... The scientific priesthood that has authority to interpret the official creation story gains immense cultural influence thereby, which it might lose if the story were called into question. The experts therefore have a vested interest in protecting the story, and in imposing rules of reasoning that make it invulnerable. When critics ask, 'Is your theory really true?' we should not be satisfied to be answered that 'it is good science, as we define science.'" (Johnson)

e. Evolutionists are not interested in testing if their theory is true. They simply believe once you ignore the creating hand of God, it is the only explanation available, so their job is to figure out how it works, not if it is true.

5. Why is the theory of evolution so universally believed today?

a. In the 1920's, a former substitute teacher in a Tennessee school volunteered to be the defendant in a case meant to challenge a state law prohibiting the teaching of evolution in the public schools. The teacher wasn't even sure he had taught evolution, but the trial went ahead.

b. Prosecuting the case was William Jennings Bryan, former Secretary of State under Woodrow Wilson, and a three-time Democratic candidate for President. Bryan believed in the Bible, but not literally. He thought the "days" of Genesis referred not to 24-hour days, but to historical ages of indefinite duration. Leading the defense was Clarence Darrow, a famous criminal lawyer, and agnostic lecturer. Darrow maneuvered Bryan to take the stand as an expert witness on the Bible, and he humiliated Bryan in a devastating cross-examination. Once that purpose was accomplished, Darrow pleaded guilty on behalf of his client and paid a $100 fine.

c. The trial was therefore inconclusive, but the "Scopes Monkey Trial" was presented to the world by sarcastic journalist H.L. Mencken, Broadway, and Hollywood, and was a huge public relations triumph for Darwinism. People who believed in God's creation came to be thought of as fools and hicks, and evolution was given the veneer of respectability. Combine this with a strong anti-supernaturalism on the part of many scientists and educators, and today's acceptance of evolution is understandable.

d. The same attitude is used to squelch debate and questions about evolution today. "When outsiders question whether the theory of evolution is as secure as we have been led to believe, we are firmly told that such questions are out of order. The arguments among the experts are said to be about matters of detail, such as the precise time scale and the mechanism of evolutionary transformations. These disagreements are signs not of crisis but of healthy creative ferment within the field, and in any case there is no room for doubt whatever about something called the 'fact' of evolution" (Johnson).

CHAPTER 2

Genesis 2:1-17 – Adam in the Garden of Eden

Genesis 25-2:18 – The Creation of Woman

The completion of creation.

1. (1-3) The seventh day of creation.

Thus the heavens and the earth, and all the host of them, were finished. And on the seventh day God ended His work which He had done, and He rested on the seventh day from all His work which He had done. Then God blessed the seventh day and sanctified it, because in it He rested from all His work which God had created and made.

a. **And He rested on the seventh day:** God did not need rest on the seventh day because He was tired. He rested to show His creating work was done, to give a pattern to man regarding the structure of time (in seven-day weeks), and to give an example of the blessing of rest to man on the seventh day.

i. The seven-day week is permanently ingrained in man. Though some through history tried to change the seven-day week (a ten-day week was attempted during the French Revolution), those attempts have come to nothing. We are on a seven-day cycle because God is on a seven-day cycle.

b. God blessed the seventh day and sanctified it: God sanctified the seventh day because it was a gift to man for rest and replenishment, and most of all because the Sabbath is a shadow of the rest available through the person and work of Jesus Christ.

i. Colossians 2:16-17 and Galatians 11-4:9 make it clear that Christians are not under obligation to observe the Sabbath today because Jesus fulfilled the purpose and plan of the Sabbath for us and in us (Hebrews 11-4:9). Yet Christians do not lose the Sabbath; every day is a day of rest in the finished work of Jesus Christ. Every day is specially set apart to God.

ii. Though we are free from the legal obligation of the Sabbath, we dare not ignore the importance of a day of rest. God has built us so we need one. But we are also commanded to work six days. "He who idles his time away in the six days is equally culpable in the sight of God as he who works on the seventh" (Clarke). In our modern world of four or five-day workweeks and generous vacation time, surely more "leisure time" can be given to the work of the LORD.

c. In it He rested from all His work: Though God rested on the seventh day of creation, He did not institute the Sabbath or show us His rest for His own sake. God does not take the Sabbath off. Jesus Himself said, My Father has been working until now, and I have been working (John 5:17). God does not need a day off, but man needs to see the rest of God and know he can enter into it by the finished work of Jesus.

i. The description of each other day of creation ended with the phrase, so the evening and the morning were the… day. However, this seventh day of creation does not have that phrase. This is because God's rest for us isn't confined to one literal day. In Jesus, God has an eternal Sabbath rest for His people (Hebrews 4:9-11).

ii. "God, having completed His work of creation, rests, as if to say, 'This is the destiny of those who are My people; to rest as I rest, to rest in Me.'"

2. (4-7) The history of the heavens and the earth.

This is the history of the heavens and the earth when they were created, in the day that the LORD God made the earth and the heavens, before any plant of the field was in the earth and before any herb of the field had grown. For the LORD God had not caused it to rain on the earth, and there was no man to till the ground; but a mist went up from the earth and watered the whole face of the ground. And the LORD God formed man of the dust of the ground, and breathed into his nostrils the breath of life; and man became a living being.

a. This is the history of the heavens and the earth: This probably ends the "genealogy" of the heavens and the earth, a history given directly by God to either Moses or Adam, recording the history of God's seven-day creation. This was something no human was present to witness.

b. In the day that the LORD God made the earth and the heavens: This is the first use of LORD (Yahweh) in the Bible. Our English word Lord comes from the Anglo-Saxon word for bread (as does our word loaf) because ancient English men of high stature would keep a continual open house, where all could come and get bread to eat. They gained the honorable title of lords, meaning "dispensers of bread."

c. Before any plant of the field was in the earth: This history begins before there was any vegetation on the earth at all (back to Genesis 1:1), a time when there were only space and a watery globe we know as the earth.

d. The LORD God had not caused it to rain on the earth: When God first created vegetation (on the third day of creation, Genesis 1:11-13), man had not yet been created to care for the vegetation of the earth, and there was no rain. The thick blanket of water vapor in the outer atmosphere created on the second day of creation (Genesis 1:6-8) made for no rain cycle (as we know it) but for a rich system of evaporation and condensation, resulting in heavy dew or ground-fog.

e. The LORD God formed man of the dust of the ground: When God created man He made him out of the most basic elements, the dust of the ground. There is nothing "spectacular" in what man is made of, only in the way those basic things are organized.

i. When the Bible uses dust in a figurative or symbolic sense, it means something of little worth, associated with lowliness and humility (Genesis 18:27; 1 Samuel 2:8; 1 Kings 16:2). In the Bible, dust isn't evil and it isn't nothing; but it is next to nothing.

f. And breathed into his nostrils the breath of life; and man became a living being: With this Divine breath, man became a living being, like other forms of animal life (the term chay nephesh is used in Genesis 1:20-21 and here). Yet only man is a living being made in the image of God (Genesis 27-1:26).

i. The word for breath in Hebrew is ruach – the word imitates the very sound of breath – is the same word for Spirit, as is the case in both ancient Greek (pneuma) and Latin (spiritus). God created man by putting His breath, His Spirit, within him.

ii. "The implication, readily seen by any Hebrew reader, [is] that man was specially created by God's breathing some of His own breath into him." (Boice)

iii. The King James Version reads: man became a living soul. This makes some wonder if man is a soul, or if man has a soul. This passage seems to indicate that man is a soul, while passages like 1 Thessalonians 5:23 and Hebrews 4:12 seem to indicate that man has a soul. It seems that the Scripture speaks in both ways, and uses the term in different ways and in different contexts.

B. Adam in the Garden of Eden.

1. (8-9) Two trees in the Garden of Eden.

The LORD God planted a garden eastward in Eden, and there He put the man whom He had formed. And out of the ground the LORD God made every tree grow that is pleasant to the sight and good for food. The tree of life was also in the midst of the garden, and the tree of the knowledge of good and evil.

a. The LORD God planted a garden eastward in Eden: Eden was a garden specifically planted by God; it was a place God made to be a perfect habitation for Adam (and later, Eve).

b. There he put the man whom He had formed: The details in the creation of Adam and Eve teach us something. After reading Genesis 1, we might have assumed that man and woman were made at the same time, but the text doesn't specifically say so. We assume it. We don't know the details about man's creation until Genesis 2.

c. Out of the ground the LORD God made every tree grow: The rest of Genesis chapter 2 does not present a different or contradictory account of creation. Rather, it is probably the history of creation from Adam's perspective. This is Adam's experience of creation, which does not contradict the account of Genesis 1:1-2:7 – it fills it out.

i. In Matthew 19:4-5, Jesus referred to events in Genesis 1 and to events in Genesis 2 as one harmonious account.

d. The tree of life… the tree of the knowledge of good and evil: These two trees were among all the other trees God created and put in the Garden of Eden.

i. The tree of life was to grant (or to sustain) eternal life (Genesis 3:22). God still has a tree of life available to His people (Revelation 2:7), which is in heaven (Revelation 22:2).

ii. The tree of the knowledge of good and evil was the "temptation" tree. Eating the fruit of this tree would give Adam an experiential knowledge of good and evil. Or, it is possible that it is called the tree of the knowledge of good and evil not so man would know good and evil, but so God could test good and evil in man.

2. (10-14) Rivers in the Garden.

Now a river went out of Eden to water the garden, and from there it parted and became four riverheads. The name of the first is Pishon; it is the one which skirts the whole land of Havilah, where there is gold. And the gold of that land is good. Bdellium and the onyx stone are there. The name of the second river is Gihon; it is the one which goes around the whole land of Cush. The name of the third river is Hiddekel; it is the one which goes toward the east of Assyria. The fourth river is the Euphrates.

a. Now a river went out of Eden: The whole feel of this account gives the sense that it was written by an actual eyewitness of the rivers and surroundings. Adam probably wrote this himself.

b. **The name of the first is Pishon:** These rivers are given specific names which answer to names of rivers known in either their modern or ancient world. However, the names of these rivers can't be used to determine the place of the Garden of Eden because the flood dramatically changed the earth's landscape and "erased" these rivers.

i. We know modern rivers today such as the Tigris or Euphrates because Noah and his sons named some rivers in the post-flood world after familiar pre-flood rivers.

3. (15-17) God's command to Adam.

Then the LORD God took the man and put him in the garden of Eden to tend and keep it. And the LORD God commanded the man, saying, "Of every tree of the garden you may freely eat; but of the tree of the knowledge of good and evil you shall not eat, for in the day that you eat of it you shall surely die."

a. **Put him in the garden of Eden to tend and keep it:** God put Adam into the most spectacular paradise the world has seen, but God put Adam there to do work (to tend and keep it). Work is something good for man and was part of Adam's perfect existence before the fall.

i. "The ideal state of sinless man is not one of indolence without responsibility. Work and duty belong to the perfect state." (Leupold)

b. **Of the tree of the knowledge of good and evil you shall not eat:** The presence of this tree – the presence of a choice for Adam – was good because for Adam to be a creature of free will, there had to be a choice, some opportunity to rebel against God. If there is never a command or never something forbidden there can then never be choice. God wants our love and obedience to Him to be the love and obedience of choice.

i. Considering all that, look at Adam's advantages. He only had one way he could sin and we have countless ways. There are many trees of temptation in our lives, but Adam had only one.

ii. God made this command originally to Adam, not to Eve; God had not yet brought woman out of man.

c. In the day that you eat of it you shall surely die: God not only made His command clear to Adam, but He also clearly explained the consequences for disobedience.

C. God creates the first woman.

1. (18) God declares He will make a helper comparable to Adam.

And the LORD God said, "It is not good that man should be alone; I will make him a helper comparable to him."

a. It is not good that man should be alone: For the first time, God saw something that was not good – the aloneness of man. God never intended for man to be alone, either in the marital or social sense.

i. Marriage, in particular, has a blessed civilizing influence on man. The wildest, most violent, sociopathic men in history have always been single, never under the plan God gave to influence men for good. For society as a whole, this is not good.

b. I will make him a helper comparable to him: God's "blueprint" for creating this companion to Adam was to make a helper comparable to Adam.

i. Different versions of the Bible translate this idea in a variety of ways, but the idea is essentially the same in each of them:

Helper meet (suitable, adapted, completing) (Amplified).

A companion… a helper suited to his needs

A helper such as he needs

A helper correspondent to himself (Septuagint Bible).

A helper suitable (NIV, NASB).

A help meet for him (KJV).

c. A helper comparable: In reference to the marriage relationship, God created woman to be a perfectly suitable helper to the man. This means God gave the plan and agenda to Adam, and he and the woman together work to fulfill it.

i. The phrase "in reference to the marriage relationship" is used because God has not ordained women to be helpers to men in authority (instead of being in authority themselves), except in marriage and in the church (1 Timothy 2:12-13).

ii. God gives to man the responsibility (and the accountability) to be the leader in the home and gives to the woman the responsibility and the accountability to help him.

iii. This does not mean there is to be no help from the man to the woman (though in many cases this is sadly true). It means when God looks down from heaven upon the family, He sees a man in leadership, good or bad, faithful or not, to the calling of leadership. A true leader will, of course, help those helping him.

iv. We only see "helping" as a position of inferiority when we think like the world thinks. God considers positions of service as most important in His sight (Matthew 20:25-28).

d. A helper comparable: Not only was the woman to be a helper but also she was made comparable to the man. She should be considered and honored as such. A woman or wife cannot be regarded as a mere tool or worker, but as an equal partner in God's grace and an equal human being.

2. (19-20) No helper was found comparable for Adam among the animals.

Out of the ground the LORD God formed every beast of the field and every bird of the air, and brought them to Adam to see what he would call them. And whatever Adam called each living creature, that was its name. So Adam gave names to all cattle, to the birds of the air, and to every beast of the field. But for Adam there was not found a helper comparable to him.

a. **Brought them to Adam to see what he would call them:** Since Adam had the capability to intelligently name all the animals, it shows he was a brilliant man. Because at this time Adam's intellect had not yet suffered from the fall, he was probably the most brilliant man who ever lived. Adam was the first and greatest of all biologists and botanists.

b. **So Adam gave names:** Adam did not name any other animal after himself, calling any other animal "man" or "human." By this, we see he understood that he was essentially different from all the animals. They were not made in the image of God.

i. Mark Twain had a joke where he described Adam coming home to Eve after naming all the animals. Eve looked at an elephant and said, "What did you name that big animal?" Adam replied, "I called it an elephant." Eve asked, "Why did you call it an elephant?" Adam answered, "Because it looked like an elephant!"

c. **But for Adam there was not found a helper:** It was obvious to Adam that the animals came in pairs and he had no mate. Since God deliberately had Adam name the animals after seeing his need for a partner (Genesis 2:18), God used this to prepare Adam to receive the gift of woman.

3. (21-22) God makes the first woman from Adam's side.

And the LORD God caused a deep sleep to fall on Adam, and he slept; and He took one of his ribs, and closed up the flesh in its place. Then the rib which the LORD God had taken from man He made into a woman, and He brought her to the man.

a. God caused a deep sleep to fall on Adam: This is the first surgery recorded in history. God even used a proper anesthetic on Adam.

b. The rib which the LORD God had taken from man He made into a woman: God used Adam's own body to create Eve to forever remind him of their essential oneness. As Adam came to know Eve he would see many ways that they were different, but he must never forget that they are essentially one and that they are made of the same substance. They are more alike than they are different.

i. We don't really know exactly what God took from Adam's side to make Eve, and it doesn't really matter. Modern research into cloning and genetic replication shows every cell in our body contains the body's entire genetic blueprint. God took some of Adam's cells and changed their genetic blueprint in the creation of Eve. Nevertheless, the story that women have one more rib than men because of the way Eve was created is a myth.

ii. We also know the Bride of Christ comes from the wound made in the side of the second Adam, Jesus Christ.

iii. There is a beautiful Jewish tradition saying God made woman, not out of man's foot to be under him, nor out of his head to be over him, but "She was taken from under his arm that he might protect her and from next to his heart that he might love her" (Barnhouse).

c. He made into a woman: It is important to realize that there are not two beginnings to the human race, one in Adam and one in Eve. There was one beginning of the human race in Adam.

d. And He brought her to the man: God brought Eve to Adam and created Eve out of Adam. He was first – the source and the head. She was created to be a helper perfectly suited to him. Thus the subordinate relationship of wives to husbands is found before the curse, not only after it.

4. (23) Adam's brilliant understanding of who Eve is and her connection to him.

And Adam said:

"This is now bone of my bones

And flesh of my flesh;

She shall be called Woman,

Because she was taken out of Man."

a. This is now bone of my bones: Adam recognized that Eve was both like him (bone of my bones and flesh of my flesh) and not like him (woman... taken out of man). They were one, but they were not the same.

b. Flesh of my flesh: Adam understood the essential oneness in his relationship with Eve. This point is so important that it is referred to several times in the New Testament, including the great marriage passage in Ephesians 5:28-29: So husbands ought to love their own wives as their own bodies; he who loves his wife loves himself. For no one ever hated his own flesh, but nourishes and cherishes it.

i. No one walks into a room and seeks the most uncomfortable seat. The natural concern we have for ourselves causes us to take care of ourselves. In a healthy marriage relationship, the husband realizes the essential union he has with his wife, and that he cannot bless her without blessing himself and he cannot mistreat or neglect her without mistreating or neglecting himself.

c. She was taken out of Man: Adam recognized that though he and Eve were one, she was not the same as him. He understood that two different people were becoming one. 1 Peter 3:7 tells husbands to recognize that they are one with someone different, someone whom they must understand: Likewise, you husbands, dwell with them with understanding, giving honor to the wife, as to the weaker vessel.

i. If men and women are different, are they equal? Elisabeth Elliot said: "In what sense is red equal to blue? They are equal only in the sense that both are colors in the spectrum. Apart from that they are different. In what sense is hot equal to cold? They are both temperatures, but beyond this it is almost meaningless to talk about equality" (cited in Boice).

ii. She shall be called woman: "Woman has been defined by many as compounded for wo and man, as if called man's wo because she tempted him to eat the forbidden fruit; but this is no meaning of the original word, nor could it be intended, as the transgression was not then committed." (Clarke)

5. (24-25) The marriage of Adam and Eve.

Therefore a man shall leave his father and mother and be joined to his wife, and they shall become one flesh. And they were both naked, the man and his wife, and were not ashamed.

a. They shall become one flesh: The marriage principle stated here is based on the dynamic of oneness yet distinction. A man and wife can truly come together in a one-flesh relationship, yet they must be joined. It is a spiritual fact, but the benefits of that oneness are not gained by accident or by chance.

b. They shall become one flesh: This passage forms the foundation for the Bible's understanding of marriage and family. Both Jesus (Matthew 19:5) and Paul (Ephesians 5:31) quoted it in reference to marriage.

i. "The institution of monogamous marriage, home, and family as the basic medium for the propagation of the race and the training of the young is so common to human history that people seldom pause to reflect on how or why such a custom came into being." (Morris)

ii. Many want to believe that the monogamous, two-parent family was invented in the 1950's by American television icons Ozzie and Harriet, but Adam and Eve are the original family. This is God's ideal family. This isn't polygamy. This isn't having a concubine. This isn't the keeping of mistresses. This isn't adultery. This isn't homosexual co-habitation. This isn't promiscuity. This isn't living together outside the marriage bond. This isn't serial marriage. This is God's ideal for the family, and even when we don't live up to it, it is still important to set it forth as God's ideal.

c. One flesh: The idea of one flesh is taken by many to be mainly a way of expressing sexual union. While sexual union is certainly related to the idea of one flesh, it is only one part of what it means to be one flesh. There are also important spiritual dimensions to one flesh.

i. Paul makes it clear the sexual union has one flesh implications even when we don't intend so, as when a man has sex with a prostitute (1 Corinthians 6:16). Husband and wife become one flesh under God's blessing. In extramarital sex, the partners become "one flesh" under God's curse.

ii. In this sense, there is no such thing as "casual sex." Every sexual relationship at least begins a oneflesh bond. The bond will either be something beautiful (like the beautiful dancing of Fred Astaire and Ginger Rogers) or it will be something distorted (like conjoined twins).

iii. It depends on whether the bonding takes place in a relationship with the right conditions: committed love, demonstrated by the marriage commitment, and a pursuit of true intimacy. Just because sex is taking place in marriage doesn't mean it is truly fulfilling God's purpose of bonding together a one-flesh relationship.

d. They shall become one flesh: Though an initial bond in a one-flesh relationship can be formed at the first sexual relationship a couple has, the fullness of what God wants to do in the one flesh relationship takes time. It has to become.

e. They were both naked, the man and his wife, and were not ashamed: Before the fall, Adam and Eve were both naked… and not ashamed. The idea of "nakedness" is far more than mere nudity. It has the sense of being totally open and exposed as a person before God and man. To be naked… and not ashamed means you have no sin, nothing to be rightly ashamed of, and nothing to hide.

i. Adam and Eve knew they were physically naked – nude – before the fall. What they did not know was a sinful, fallen condition, because they were not in that condition before their rebellion.

ii. We often feel uncomfortable when someone stares at us. This is because we associate staring with prying, and we don't want people to pry into our lives. We want to remain hidden and only reveal to other people what we want to reveal.

iii. When we want to be most attractive to someone else, we do the most to change our normal appearance. We have the thought, "If I really want to impress this person, I have to fix myself up." None of this feeling was present with Adam and Eve when they were naked… and not ashamed.

BIBLIOGRAPHY

Genesis 3 – Man's Temptation and Fall

Videos for Genesis 3:

Genesis 3:1-9 – Man's Temptation and Fall

Genesis 24-3:10 – Sin's Confrontation and Curse

The temptation from the serpent.

(1) The serpent begins his temptation.

Now the serpent was more cunning than any beast of the field which the LORD God had made. And he said to the woman, "Has God indeed said, 'You shall not eat of every tree of the garden'?"

a. The serpent: The text here does not, by itself alone, clearly identify the serpent as Satan, but the rest of the Bible makes it clear this is Satan appearing as a serpent.

    i. In Ezekiel 28:13-19 tells us that Satan was in Eden. Many other passages associate a serpent or a snake-like creature with Satan (such as Job 26:13 and Isaiah 51:9). Revelation 12:9 and 20:2 speak of the dragon, that serpent of old, who is the Devil and Satan.

    ii. The representation of Satan as a serpent makes the idea of Moses saving Israel by lifting up a bronze serpent all the more provocative (Numbers

21:8-9), especially when Jesus identifies Himself with that very serpent (John 3:14). This is because, in this picture, the serpent (a personification of sin and rebellion) is made of bronze (a metal associated with judgment, since it is made with fire). The lifting of a bronze serpent is the lifting up of sin judged, in the form of a cross.

iii. Ezekiel 28 tells us Satan, before his fall, was an angel of the highest rank and prominence, even something of a leader of worship in heaven. Isaiah 14 tells us Satan's fall had to do with his desire to be equal to or greater than God, to set his will against God's will.

iv. We may not understand everything involved in the way Satan used the body of a serpent, but we can know it was true and this is no mere fable. "It is idle to call the narrative of the Fall a mere allegory; one had better say at once that he does not believe the Book... There was a real serpent, as there was a real paradise; there was a real Adam and Eve, who stood at the head of our race, and they really sinned, and our race is really fallen. Believe this" (Spurgeon).

b. The serpent was more cunning than any beast: Satan's effectiveness is often found in His cunning, crafty ways. We can't outsmart Satan, but we can overcome him with the power of Jesus.

i. It was the craftiness of Satan that made him successful against Eve: as the serpent deceived Eve by his craftiness (2 Corinthians 11:3).

ii. "Man has, perhaps, far more cunning than any mere creature… but Satan has more of cunning within him than any other creature that the Lord God hath made, man included." (Spurgeon)

c. And he said to the woman: Apparently, before the curse pronounced in Genesis 3:14-15, the serpent was different than what we know today as a serpent. This creature didn't start as a snake as we know it, it became one.

i. "In all probability the reptile called the serpent was a nobler creature before the Fall than now. The words of our text, so far as they literally concern the serpent, threaten that a change would be wrought in him. It has been a sort of speculative opinion that the creature either had wings, or was able to move without creeping upon the earth as it now does." (Spurgeon)

ii. Demonic spirits evidently have the ability, under certain circumstances, to indwell human or animal bodies (Luke 8:33). On this occasion, Satan chose to indwell the body of a pre-curse serpent. "An immaterial spirit must be invisible; and therefore he must embody himself in some way or other before he can be seen. That Satan has power to enter into living bodies is clear, for he did so upon a very large scale with regard to men in the days of Christ… Being compelled to have an embodiment, the master evil spirit perceived the serpent to be at that time among the most subtle of all creatures; and therefore he entered into the serpent as feeling that he would be most at home in that animal" (Spurgeon).

iii. Poole says the woman wasn't surprised at the serpent's speaking because Adam and Eve had free conversation with angelic beings that often appeared in the form of men. If this is true, it wasn't so strange to Eve that an angelic being might appear to her in the form of a beautiful pre-curse serpent.

iv. Perhaps Satan made the voice supernaturally seem to come forth from the serpent, or perhaps Satan communicated this to Eve in her thoughts. What Satan said is more important than how he said it.

d. To the woman: Satan brought his temptation against the woman because he perceived she was more vulnerable to attack. This is because she did not receive the command to not eat of the tree of the knowledge of good and evil directly from God but through Adam (Genesis 2:15-17).

i. Perhaps Satan knew by observation Adam didn't do an effective job of communicating to Eve what the LORD told him. This failure on Adam's part made Eve more vulnerable to temptation.

ii. Satan will often attack a chain at its weakest link, so he gets at Adam by tempting Eve. The stronger ones in a "chain" must expect an attack against weaker links and support them against those attacks.

iii. It was also in God's plan to allow Satan to tempt Eve this way. If Adam would have sinned first, and if he had then given the fruit to Eve, she might have a partial excuse before God: "I was simply obeying the head of our home. When he gave me the fruit, I ate of it."

e. Has God indeed said: Satan's first attack was leveled against the Word of God. If he could make Eve confused about what God said, or to doubt what God said, then his battle was partially won.

i. From the beginning, Satan has tried to undermine God's people by undermining God's Word. He can undermine just as effectively by getting us to neglect God's Word as by getting us to doubt it.

e. Has God indeed said, "You shall not eat of every tree of the garden"? Satan took God's positive command in Genesis 2:16-17 (Of every tree of the garden you may freely eat; but of the tree of the knowledge of good and evil you shall not eat) and rephrased it in a purely negative way: "God won't let you eat of every tree."

2. (2-3) Eve's reply to the serpent.

And the woman said to the serpent, "We may eat the fruit of the trees of the garden; but of the fruit of the tree which is in the midst of the garden, God has said, 'You shall not eat it, nor shall you touch it, lest you die.'"

a. And the woman said to the serpent: Eve's first mistake was in even carrying on a discussion with the serpent. We are called to talk to the devil, but never to have a discussion with him. We simply and strongly tell him, "The Lord rebuke you!" (Jude 9).

b. **We may eat of the fruit of the trees of the garden:** Eve's knowledge of what she should not do is partially correct, but what she doesn't seem to know makes her all the more vulnerable to deception.

i. Eve does not seem to know the name of this tree; she only calls it **the tree in the midst of the garden,** instead of the tree of the knowledge of good and evil (Genesis 2:17).

ii. Eve misquoted God's command to Adam. Her words, **you shall not eat it** and **lest you die** are close enough, but she added to the command and put words in God's mouth when she said, **nor shall you touch it.** Of course, it was a good idea to completely avoid the temptation; no good could come from massaging the fruit you're not supposed to eat. But it is a dangerous thing to teach the doctrines of man as if they are the commandments of God (Matthew 15:9).

iii. Clarke on **nor shall you touch it:** "Some Jewish writers… state that as soon as the woman had asserted this, the serpent pushed her against the tree and said, 'See, you have touched it, and are still alive; you may therefore safely eat of the fruit, for surely you shall not die.'"

c. **God has said:** Eve's ignorance of exactly what God said was really Adam's responsibility. He did a poor job of relating to his wife the word God gave him.

i. We can almost picture Adam telling Eve, "See that tree in the middle of the garden? Don't touch it or God says we'll die!" While this is better than saying nothing, what Adam didn't explain made a vulnerable place where Satan could attack.

d. Lest you die: This may seem like a small thing to hinge the destiny of the human race and all creation on. But the tree was nothing more than a restraint on Adam and Eve. It reminded them they were not God, that God had a legitimate claim to their obedience, and that they were responsible to Him.

3. (4-5) Satan's direct challenge to God's Word.

Then the serpent said to the woman, "You will not surely die. For God knows that in the day you eat of it your eyes will be opened, and you will be like God, knowing good and evil."

a. You will not surely die: Satan effectively laid the groundwork. He drew Eve into a discussion with him and planted the seed of doubt about God's Word, and he exposed Eve's incomplete understanding of God's Word. Now he moves in for the kill, with an outright contradiction of what God said.

i. Satan can only effectively work when he has established a foothold. No one falls like Adam and Eve will fall, "all of a sudden." A foundation has been laid.

ii. This is why we are called to never give place to the devil (Ephesians 4:27). This shows how remarkable it is that Jesus could say, "Satan has nothing in Me" (John 14:30).

b. **You will not surely die:** Satan first wanted Eve to forget all about what God said about the consequences of sin. When we know and remember the consequences of sin, we are more likely to give up the passing pleasures of sin (Hebrews 11:25).

    i. In Satan's direct challenge, he tries to get Eve to doubt the goodness of God. If God lies to her, how can He be good?

    ii. In Satan's direct challenge, he tries to get Eve to doubt the badness of sin. If this fruit is something good for her, why doesn't God want her to have it?

    iii. Satan wants us to see sin as something good that a bad God doesn't want us to have. His main lie to us is "sin is not bad, and God is not good."

    iv. "Satan and the flesh will present a thousand reasons to show how good it would be to disobey His command." (Barnhouse)

c. **In the day you eat of it your eyes will be opened:** Satan's temptation was all the more powerful because there was truth in it. It was true your eyes will be opened, and this was fulfilled (Genesis 3:7). But their eyes were instantly opened to their own sin and rebellion.

    i. It is as if a deaf person was promised to be able to hear again, but all they could hear was screaming.

    ii. Their eyes were opened, they did know good and evil, but not as gods. A complete lie is rarely effective in temptation. If Satan doesn't couple it with some truth, there is little power in his temptation.

d. You will be like God, knowing good and evil: The final enticement was the most powerful because it was how Satan himself fell, wanting to be equal with God. Eve tried to become a god by rebelling against God.

i. Jewish rabbis embellished on Satan's temptation to Eve: "Nothing but malice has prompted God's command, because as soon as you eat of it, you will be as God. As He creates and destroys worlds, so will you have the power to create and destroy. As He does kill and revive, so will you have the power to kill and revive. God Himself ate first of the fruit of the tree, and then He created the world. Therefore, He forbids you to eat of it, lest you create other worlds... Hurry now and eat the fruit of the tree in the midst of the garden, and become independent of God, lest He bring forth still other creatures that will rule over you" (Ginzberg).

ii. The goal of becoming God is the center of so many non-Christian religions, including Mormonism. But in our desire to be gods, we become like Satan. It was Satan who said, I will ascend into heaven, I will exalt my throne above the stars of God... I will be like the Most High (Isaiah 14:13-14). In contrast, we should be like Jesus, who came as a servant (Matthew 20:28).

iii. The New Age movement and the desire to be "god" are just as strong as ever. According to a 1992 survey, as many as 12 million Americans can be considered active participants in the New Age movement, and another 30 million are avidly interested. If all these people were brought together in a church-like organization, it would be the third largest religious denomination in America. More than 90% of the subscribers to New Age Magazine are college graduates, compared to half the general population.

iv. In 1995, New Age influence made it all the way to the White House. New Age author Marianne Williamson (author of A Return to Love: Reflections on the Principles of A Course in Miracles), guru to many of Hollywood's spiritual seekers, spent a night at the White House as the personal guest of Hillary Clinton. Anthony Robbins, motivational guru and king of latenight infomercials, consulted with President Clinton at Camp David. Robbins is also recognized as a leader in the New Age movement.

B. The sin of Adam and Eve and the fall of the human race.

1. (6) Adam and Eve both disobey God in their own way.

So when the woman saw that the tree was good for food, that it was pleasant to the eyes, and a tree desirable to make one wise, she took of its fruit and ate. She also gave to her husband with her, and he ate.

a. So when the woman saw: Eve surrendered to this temptation in exactly the way John describes in 1 John 2:16. First, she gave in to the lust of the flesh (saw that it was good for food), then she gave in to the lust of the eyes (pleasant to the eyes), then she gave in to the pride of life (desirable to make one wise).

    i. Jesus was tempted in the same three-fold way: an appeal to the physical appetites, an appeal to covetous and emotional desires, and an appeal to pride (Matthew 4:1-11).

b. The woman saw that the tree was good for food: Eve's perceptions were partially true and partially false. The tree was not really good for food, though Eve was deceived into thinking it was so. The fruit probably was pleasant to the eyes, though that shouldn't mean much. And it was only true in Eve's mind that the tree was desirable to make one wise.

    i. We can see the precise truth of Paul's statement in 1 Timothy 2:14, that Eve was deceived when she sinned. In her mind, she thought she was doing something good for herself.

c. She took of its fruit and ate: Satan could tempt Eve, but she didn't have to take it. The taking was all her doing. Satan couldn't cram the fruit down her throat. Eve was responsible. She couldn't rightly say, "the devil made me do it."

    i. As with every temptation, God had made for Eve a way of escape (1 Corinthians 10:13). She could have simply run from Satan and the tree, but Eve didn't take God's way of escape.

d. She also gave to her husband with her: Not only did Eve sin, but also she became the agent of temptation for Adam. But when Adam ate, he was not deceived as Eve was. Adam sinned with his eyes wide open, in open rebellion against God.

i. Therefore, it is Adam and not Eve who bears the responsibility for the fall of the human race and for the introduction of death into the created order (Romans 5:12, 1 Corinthians 15:22). Eve was tricked into sinning; Adam knew exactly what he was doing (1 Timothy 2:14).

ii. Many have speculated that Adam sinned because he didn't want Eve to be alone in the fall, and he ate of the fruit out of a romantic impulse. This may well be true, but it makes Adam's sin not one bit less rebellious. Rebellion against God is not "better" when motivated by a romantic impulse.

iii. "Take and eat" will one day become verbs of salvation, but only after Jesus had lived in the world of Adam's curse and surrendered to death.

2. (7) The nakedness of Adam and Eve.

Then the eyes of both of them were opened, and they knew that they were naked; and they sewed fig leaves together and made themselves coverings.

a. Then the eyes of both of them were opened: Seemingly, it was only after the sin of Adam that they knew of their sinful state. They knew they were naked, in the sense of having their shame exposed to all creation.

b. They knew that they were naked: Both Psalm 104:2 and Matthew 17:2 suggest that light can be a garment for the righteous. It may be that Adam and Eve were previously clothed in God's glorious light, and the immediate loss of this covering of light left them feeling exposed and naked.

i. "It is more than probable that they were clothed in light before the fall, and when they sinned the light went out." (Barnhouse)

c. The eyes of both of them were opened: The way they saw themselves changed, but also the way they saw the entire world was now different. After the fall, everything looked worse.

i. When Adam and Eve saw their nakedness and felt terrible about it, it didn't feel good but it was good. It is good to feel guilty when you have done something wrong, and having no sense of guilt or shame is worse.

d. They sewed fig leaves together: Their own attempt to cover themselves took much ingenuity, but not much wisdom. Fig leaves have something of a prickly quality, which would make for some pretty itchy coverings.

i. Every attempt to cover our own nakedness before God is just as foolish. We need to let Jesus cover us (Revelation 3:5, 18), and put on Jesus Himself as our covering garment (Galatians 3:27). God has a covering for His people (Isaiah 61:10), and the exhortation from Jesus is for us: Behold, I am coming as a thief. Blessed is he who watches, and keeps his garments, lest he walk naked and they see his shame (Revelation 16:15).

ii. Obviously, they covered their genital areas. In virtually all cultures, adults cover their genital areas, even though other parts of the human body may be more or less exposed from culture to culture.

iii. This is not because there is something intrinsically unclean in our sexuality, but because we have both received our fallenness and pass it on genetically through sexual reproduction. Because of this, God has implanted it in the minds of men that more modesty is appropriate for these areas of our body.

e. Made themselves coverings: After making their coverings, Adam and Eve waited. It would not be until the cool of the day (Genesis 3:8) when God would normally come to them. With anxiety and perhaps a bit of agony they waited until God patiently came to them.

i. "Their hearts must have been sorely perplexed within them while they were waiting to see what God would do to them as a punishment for the great sin they had committed." (Spurgeon)

3. (8-9) Adam and Eve hide from God; God calls out to them.

And they heard the sound of the LORD God walking in the garden in the cool of the day, and Adam and his wife hid themselves from the presence of the

LORD God among the trees of the garden. Then the LORD God called to Adam and said to him, "Where are you?"

a. They heard the sound of the LORD God walking in the garden in the cool of the day: Adam and Eve knew that when they heard the LORD coming, He would want to be with them. This was how the LORD had fellowship with Adam and Eve, in a very natural, close, intimate way.

i. Leupold on walking in the garden in the cool of the day: "The almost casual way in which this is remarked indicates that this did not occur for the first time just then... There is extreme likelihood that the Almighty assumed some form analogous to the human form which was made in His image."

ii. We can assume this is God, in the Person of Jesus Christ, appearing to Adam and Eve before His incarnation and birth at Bethlehem, because of God the Father it is said, "No one has seen God at any time. The only begotten Son, who is in the bosom of the Father, He has declared Him" (John 1:18); and no man has ever seen God in the Person of the Father (1 Timothy 6:16).

iii. Cool of the day is literally "the breeze of the day." From Hebrew geography and culture, we might guess this means late afternoon or early evening. Charles Spurgeon thought the sense was, "in the wind of the evening," when the evening breeze was blowing through the garden.

iv. "Not in the dead of night when the natural glooms of darkness might have increased the terrors of the criminal, not in the heat of the day, lest he should imagine that God come in the heat of passion; not in the early morning, as if in haste to slay, but at the close of the day, for God is long-suffering, slow to anger, and of great mercy." (Spurgeon)

b. Adam and his wife hid themselves: This shows that Adam and Eve knew that their attempt to cover themselves failed. They didn't proudly show off their fig-leaf outfits; they knew their own covering was completely inadequate, and they were embarrassed before God.

c. Where are you? This was not the interrogation of an angry commanding officer, but the heartfelt cry of an anguished father. God obviously knew where they were but He also knew a gulf had been made between Him and man, a gulf that He Himself would have to bridge.

The question was meant to arouse Adam's sense of being lost.

The question was meant to lead Adam to confess his sin.

The question was meant to express God's sorrow over man's lost condition.

The question was meant to show that God seeks after lost man.

The question was meant to express the accountability man had before God.

i. God's question demanded an answer. They couldn't refuse to answer God the way a criminal might keep silent when questioned. "In our courts of law, we do not require men to answer questions which would incriminate them, but God does; and, at the last great day, the ungodly will be condemned on their own confession of guilt" (Spurgeon).

ii. The way God came to Adam and Eve is a model of how He comes to lost and fallen humanity ever since.

God came to them patiently, waiting for the cool of the day – the evening time.

God came to them with care, coming before the darkness of night.

God came to them personally, addressing Adam and Eve directly.

God came to them with truth, showing them their lost condition.

God confronts Adam and Eve with their sin.

1. (10-12) Adam tries to explain his sin.

So he said, "I heard Your voice in the garden, and I was afraid because I was naked; and I hid myself." And He said, "Who told you that you were naked? Have you eaten from the tree of which I commanded you that you should not eat?" Then the man said, "The woman whom You gave to be with me, she gave me of the tree, and I ate."

a. I heard Your voice in the garden, and I was afraid: Sin made Adam afraid of God's presence and afraid of God's voice. Ever since Adam, men run from God's presence and don't want to listen to His Word.

    i. We are still made in God's image, so we want to be in the presence of God and hear His voice, while at the same time, we are afraid of Him.

b. **Who told you that you were naked?** God knew the answer to this question. He asked it because He allowed Adam to make the best of a bad situation by repenting right then and there, but Adam didn't come clean and repent before God.

    i. We all sin, but when we sin, we can still give glory to God by openly confessing without shifting the blame onto others (Joshua 7:19-20).

    ii. There is often nothing you can do about yesterday's sin (though in some cases you may be able to make restitution). Yet you can do what is right before God right now by confessing and repenting.

c. **Have you eaten from the tree of which I commanded you that you should not eat?** God confronted Adam's problem squarely. This wasn't primarily a wardrobe problem or a fear problem or a self-esteem problem. This was a sin problem and Adam's wardrobe, fear or self-understanding could not be addressed until the sin problem was addressed.

d. **Then the man said:** Notice that to this point, God has not addressed Eve at all. Adam, being the head, is the problem here.

e. The woman whom You gave to be with me, she gave me of the tree, and I ate: Adam's attempt to blame Eve is completely consistent with human nature. Few of us are willing to simply say as David did, I have sinned against the LORD (2 Samuel 12:13).

i. Significantly, if there is any blame, it is on Adam, not Eve. Not only does Adam unjustly accuse Eve, but also he refused to accept proper responsibility for his part in her sin.

ii. By saying the woman whom You gave to be with me, Adam essentially blamed God for the sin saying, "You gave me the woman, and she is the problem." Adam wasn't content to blame Eve; he had to blame God also.

iii. "He was guilty of unkindness to his wife and of blasphemy against his maker, in seeking to escape from confessing the sin which he had committed. It is an ill sign with men when they cannot be brought frankly to acknowledge their wrong-doing."

2. (13) Eve's reply to God.

And the LORD God said to the woman, "What is this you have done?" The woman said, "The serpent deceived me, and I ate."

a. The serpent deceived me, and I ate: When confronted by God, Eve didn't necessarily shift the blame when she admitted the serpent deceived her and then she ate. This much was true: she had been deceived, and she did eat.

b. Deceived me: The problem comes when we fail to see that being deceived is sin in itself. It is sin to exchange the truth of God for the lie (Romans 1:25).

D. The curse and its aftermath.

1. (14-15) God's curse upon the serpent.

So the LORD God said to the serpent:

"Because you have done this,

You are cursed more than all cattle,

And more than every beast of the field;

On your belly you shall go,

And you shall eat dust

All the days of your life.

And I will put enmity

Between you and the woman,

And between your seed and her Seed;

He shall bruise your head,

And you shall bruise His heel."

a. And the LORD God said to the serpent: When God spoke to Adam and to Eve, He questioned each of them. God didn't ask Satan (the being animating the serpent) any questions because there was nothing to teach him.

i. "The Lord God did not ask the serpent anything, for he knew that he was a liar, but he at once pronounced sentence upon him." (Spurgeon)

b. **You are cursed more than all cattle:** The first part of the curse is directed at the animal that Satan used to bring the temptation. God commanded the serpent to slither on the ground instead of walking on legs like any other animal.

i. "The creature that tempted Eve became a serpent as a result of God's judgment on it, and it went slithering away into the bushes." (Boice)

ii. Adam and Eve must have been terrified as this once-beautiful creature called a serpent was transformed into the creeping, slithering, hissing snake we know today. They must have thought, "It's our turn next!"

iii. **I will put enmity between you and the woman:** In addition, there is a natural aversion between mankind and serpents, especially on the part of women.

c. **On your belly you shall go:** Whatever noble bearing the creation known as the serpent had before the fall and the curse, that nobility was gone. Now the creature Satan used to tempt Eve would be a low, groveling creature.

i. "Beings engaged in evil designs have no other way of going, but with tricks, devices, concealments, double meanings. When men deny the Scriptures and the truth of God, they always go to work in an underhand, mean, and serpentine style: 'Upon thy belly shalt thou go.' If guilty man begins to plot for his own advantage, scheme for his own glory, and aim at perverting the truth, you will notice that he never takes a bold, open, manly stand, but he dodges, he conceals, he twists and shifts: 'Upon thy belly shalt thou go.' Sin is a mean and despicable thing. The greatest potentate of evil was here doomed to cringe and crawl, and his seed have never forgotten their father's posture." (Spurgeon)

d. **You shall eat dust all the days of your life:** This was true of the serpent as an animal, but it is also true of Satan. To eat dust has the idea of total defeat (Isaiah 65:25, Micah 7:17). God's judgment on Satan is for him to always know defeat. He will always reach for victory but always fall short of it.

i. Satan was, in his own thinking, majestic and triumphant over Jesus on the cross, but he failed. In attacking Jesus, Satan made his own doom certain.

ii. In Jesus, we share in the victory over Satan: And the God of peace will crush Satan under your feet shortly (Romans 16:20).

e. **Enmity between you and the woman, and between your seed and her Seed:** The second part of the curse is directed against Satan himself. God placed a natural animosity between Satan and mankind. Enmity has the idea of ill will, hatred, and a mutual antagonism. Satan's hatred of Eve was nothing new; it was already present – but now man will, generally speaking, have antagonism towards Satan.

i. The friendship Eve and the serpent seemed to enjoy earlier in the chapter is finished. There is now a natural fear of Satan in the heart of man.

ii. If we are born naturally rebellious against God, we are also born cautious and afraid of Satan. One must be hardened to willingly and knowingly serve Satan. Instinctively, we don't serve God or Satan; we serve ourselves (which is fine with Satan).

f. He shall bruise your head, and you shall bruise His heel: In this, God prophesies the doom of Satan, showing that the real battle is between Satan and the Seed of the Woman.

i. There is no doubt this is a prophecy of Jesus' ultimate defeat of Satan. God announced that Satan would wound the Messiah (you shall bruise His heel), but the Messiah would crush Satan with a mortal wound (He shall bruise your head). It was as if God could not wait to announce His plan of salvation, to bring deliverance through the one known as the Seed of the woman.

ii. The heel is the part within the serpent's reach. Jesus, in taking on humanity, brought Himself near to Satan's domain so Satan could strike Him. "That bruised heel is painful enough. Behold our Lord in his human nature sore bruised: he was betrayed, bound, accused, buffeted, scourged, spit upon. He was nailed to the cross; he hung there in thirst and fever, and darkness and desertion" (Spurgeon).

iii. This prophecy also gives the first hint of the virgin birth, declaring the Messiah – the Deliverer – would be the Seed of the Woman, but not of the man.

iv. Genesis 3:15 has been called the protoevangelium, the first gospel. Martin Luther said of this verse: "This text embraces and comprehends within itself everything noble and glorious that is to be found anywhere in the Scriptures" (Leupold).

v. "This is the first gospel sermon that was ever delivered upon the surface of this earth. It was a memorable discourse indeed, with Jehovah himself for the preacher, and the whole human race and the prince of darkness for the audience." (Spurgeon)

g. He shall bruise your head: For God to see the defeat of Satan at Satan's first flush of victory shows God knew what He was doing all along. God's plan wasn't defeated when Adam and Eve sinned because God's plan was to bring forth something greater than man in the innocence of Eden. God wanted more than innocent man; His plan is to bring forth redeemed man.

i. Redeemed man – this being who is greater than innocent man – is only possible because man had something to be redeemed from.

2. (16) God's curse upon the woman. To the woman He said:

"I will greatly multiply your sorrow and your conception; In pain you shall bring forth children; Your desire shall be for your husband, And he shall rule over you."

a. I will greatly multiply your sorrow: God first cursed the woman with multiplied sorrow. Men and women have each known sorrow throughout history, yet the unique sorrow of women is well known.

i. Under Jesus, some of the effects of the curse are relieved, and it has been the Christianizing of society that brought rights and dignity to women.

ii. "It is difficult for women in Christian lands to realize the miseries of their hundreds of millions of sisters in pagan lands, where the lot of women is little above that of cattle. Where the gospel has gone, the load has been lifted, and woman in Christ has become the reflection of the redeemed Church, the bride of Christ." (Barnhouse)

b. Your sorrow and your conception; in pain you shall bring forth children: The first curse upon women is a broad one. It has the idea that women would experience pain in regard to their children in general, not just in the act of giving birth. God ordained that the pain with which women bring children into this world be an example of the pain they experience more generally in life.

i. It has been observed that women bring forth children with more pain than just about any other creature.

c. Your desire shall be for your husband: This is true of women in a way that it is not true for men. Barnhouse explained: "This verse will be understood better when it is realized that the desire of man toward his wife alone is solely by God's grace and not by nature."

d. **Your desire shall be for your husband, and he shall rule over you:** The idea is to contrast the woman's desire and the husband's rule over her. This speaks of an inherent challenge in embracing the husband's role as leader of the home and family.

> i. This same word for desire is used in Genesis 4:7 of the desire of sin to master over Cain. Because of the curse, Eve would have to fight a desire to master her husband, a desire that works against God's ordained order for the home.

> ii. The principle of Adam's headship as a husband was established before the fall (see Genesis 2:18 and 2:22). Now the curse on Eve makes it much harder for her to submit and flow with God's institution of male headship in the home.

> iii. "As a result of the fall, man no longer rules easily; he must fight from his headship. Sin has corrupted both the willing submission of the wife and the loving headship of the husband. The woman's desire is to control her husband (to usurp his divinely appointed headship), and he must master her, if he can. So the rule of love founded in paradise is replaced by struggle, tyranny and domination." (Susan T. Foh, cited in Boice)

3. (17-19) God's curse upon the man.

Then to Adam He said, "Because you have heeded the voice of your wife, and have eaten from the tree of which I commanded you, saying, 'You shall not eat of it':

"Cursed is the ground for your sake;

In toil you shall eat of it

All the days of your life.

Both thorns and thistles it shall bring forth for you,

And you shall eat the herb of the field.

In the sweat of your face you shall eat bread

Till you return to the ground,

For out of it you were taken;

For dust you are,

And to dust you shall return."

a. Because you have heeded the voice of your wife: It wasn't just as if Adam took Eve's advice. He chose to be with Eve instead of obeying God. There is a sense in which idolatry of Eve was an aspect of Adam's disobedience against God.

b. Cursed is the ground: Because of Adam, there is a curse upon all creation. Before the curse on man, the ground only produced good. After the curse, it still produced good, but thorns and thistles will come faster and easier than good fruit.

i. The curse promised thorns and thistles, and we remember that Jesus was crowned with thorns (Matthew 27:29). In this vivid way, Jesus bore the curse for us. "This curse of the earth was on his head, and wounded him full sore. Was he crowned with thorns, and do you wonder that they grow up around your feet? Rather bless him that ever he should have consecrated the thorns by wearing them for his diadem" (Spurgeon).

c. In toil you shall eat of it: Adam worked before the curse, but it was all joy. Now work has a cursed element to it, with pain and weariness a part of work. Is there not a time of hard service for man on earth? Are not his days also like the days of a hired man? Like a servant who earnestly desires the shade, and like a hired man who eagerly looks for his wages (Job 7:1-2).

i. "Although the sentence took away from Adam the luscious fruits of paradise, yet it secured him a livelihood. He was to live; the ground was to bring forth enough of the herb of the field for him to continue to exist. Albeit that henceforth all he ate was to be with the sweat of his face, yet still he was to have enough to eat, and he was to live on." (Spurgeon)

d. Dust you are, and to dust you shall return: The final curse upon man promised there would be an end of his toil and labor on the earth – but it was an end of death, not an end of deliverance.

i. The curse of death shows that the result of Adam's sin extended to the entire human race. Because of Adam:

Sin entered the world (Romans 5:12).

Death came to all mankind (Romans 5:15, 1 Corinthians 15:22).

Death reigned over man and creation (Romans 5:17)

All men were condemned (Romans 5:18).

All men were made sinners (Romans 5:19).

ii. The principle of Galatians 3:13 is established as we consider that Jesus bore each aspect of the curse upon Adam and Eve in its totality: Christ has redeemed us from the curse of the law, having become a curse for us.

Sin brought pain to childbirth, and no one knew more pain than Jesus did when He, through His suffering, brought many sons to glory (Hebrews 2:10).

Sin brought conflict, and Jesus endured great conflict to bring our salvation (Hebrews 12:3).

Thorns came with sin and the fall, and Jesus endured a crown of thorns to bring our salvation (John 19:2).

Sin brought sweat, and Jesus sweat, as it were, great drops of blood to win our salvation (Luke 22:44).

Sin brought sorrow, and Jesus became a man of sorrows, acquainted with grief, to save us (Isaiah 53:3).

Sin brought death, and Jesus tasted death for everyone that we might be saved (Hebrews 2:9).

2. (20) The naming of Eve.

And Adam called his wife's name Eve, because she was the mother of all living.

a. Adam called his wife's name Eve: Up to Genesis 3:20, the woman has never been called Eve. We are so used to saying "Adam and Eve" that we assume she already had her name. But to this point, she was called a female (Genesis 1:27), a helper comparable (Genesis 2:18), a woman (Genesis 2:22, 23), and a wife (Genesis 2:24, 25; 3:8). This does not mean God did not have a name for Eve, but we are told what the name is in Genesis 5:2: He called them Mankind.

i. The idea that the woman takes her name from the husband, and the idea that both genders are encompassed in terms like mankind, humanity, and chairman. Our use of these terms is not merely cultural, it is Biblical.

ii. A woman gains more of her identity from her husband than the man does from the wife. For this reason, women should take special care in which man they marry.

b. Because she was the mother of all living: Adam named her Eve, even though she was not a mother at all at the time. She was not even pregnant yet. Adam named her in faith, trusting God would bring forth a deliverer from the woman because God said He would defeat Satan through the Seed of the woman (Genesis 3:15).

i. "She was not a mother at all, but as the life was to come through her by virtue of the promised seed, Adam marks his full conviction of the truth of the promise though at the time the woman had borne no children." (Spurgeon)

5. (21) God clothes Adam and Eve in the skins of animals.

Also for Adam and his wife the LORD God made tunics of skin, and clothed them.

a. The LORD God made tunics of skin, and clothed them: God wanted Adam and Eve clothed, not naked. If nudity represented a higher, freer life, then God would have let Adam and Eve remain naked – but He clothed them.

    i. "God gave His approval of the sense of shame which had led our first parents to cover their nakedness." (Leupold)

b. Tunics of skin: In order for Adam and Eve to be clothed, a sacrifice had to be made. An animal had to die. Without shedding of blood there is no remission of sins (Hebrews 9:22).

    i. "Some creature had to die in order to provide them with garments, and you know who it is that died in order that we might be robed in his spotless righteousness. The Lamb of God has made for us a garment which covers our nakedness so that we are not afraid to stand even before the bar of God." (Spurgeon)

    ii. There are only two religions; there is the religion of fig leaves and there is the religion of God's perfect provision through Jesus. Covering ourselves with our good works is like Adam and Eve trying to cover themselves with fig leaves. Our good works are like monopoly money – great for monopoly, but not legal tender. Your good works are essential to what it takes to live out your life, but they are not legal tender before God.

    iii. Adam and Eve were clothed with a garment that was purchased with the life of another. We are clothed with a garment of righteousness that was purchased with the life of another, Jesus Christ.

c. And clothed them: This, together with the expression of faith in God's promise indicated in the naming of Eve (Genesis 3:20), indicates that Adam and Eve were rescued from their sinful condition. Adam had faith in God's promise of a Savior, and God provided a covering for them through a sacrifice. We will see Adam and Eve in heaven.

6. (22-24) God sets cherubim to guard the Tree of Life.

Then the LORD God said, "Behold, the man has become like one of Us, to know good and evil. And now, lest he put out his hand and take also of the tree of life, and eat, and live forever"—therefore the LORD God sent him out of the garden of Eden to till the ground from which he was taken. So He drove out the man; and He placed cherubim at the east of the garden of Eden, and a flaming sword which turned every way, to guard the way to the tree of life.

a. Behold, the man has become like one of Us, to know good and evil: The idea behind this phrase is difficult to understand. Perhaps there is a note of sarcasm by God here (as Elijah used in 1 Kings 18:27), regarding Satan's empty promise to become like gods. Or, perhaps the idea focuses on man's greater knowledge (though in a bad sense) now that he has the experiential knowledge of evil.

b. And take also of the tree of life, and eat, and live forever: In mercy, God protected Adam and Eve from the horrible fate of having to live forever as sinners by preventing them from eating from the tree of life.

c. The LORD God sent him out of the garden of Eden: We don't know if Adam and Eve wanted to stay in the garden of Eden. Perhaps they felt if they left the garden, they might never see God again because it was the only place where they met Him.

d. He drove out the man; and He placed cherubim at the east of the garden of Eden: Cherubim are always associated with the presence and glory of God (Ezekiel 10, Isaiah 6, Revelation 4). When cherubim are represented on earth (such as in the tabernacle, Exodus 25:10-22), they mark a meeting place with God. Though Adam and Eve and their descendants were prevented from eating the fruit of the tree of life (by God's mercy), they could still come there to meet God. This was their "holy of holies." Therefore, it was important to send cherubim and a flaming sword to guard the way to the tree of life.

i. "Any angel of the lowest rank could have dealt with Adam. The flaming sword was pointed against Satan to keep him from destroying the way of access to the altar, which God had set up." (Barnhouse)

ii. This is the last historical mention of the garden of Eden in the Bible. We can speculate that God did not destroy it, but left it to the effects of the curse and suppose that it generally deteriorated from its original condition, blending into the surrounding geography.

CONCLUSION

Pray that you get a better understanding of the Word of God as you continue to study..

REFERENCES

Holy Bible

Enduring Word Bible Commentary

John Whesley

C.S. Francis

Carson

Matthew Poole

NOTES

BOOK:_____

CHAPTER:_____

BOOK:_____

CHAPTER:_____

BOOK:_____

CHAPTER:_____

BOOK:_____

CHAPTER:_____

BOOK:_____

CHAPTER:_____

BOOK:_____

CHAPTER:_____

BOOK:_____

CHAPTER:_____

BOOK:_____

CHAPTER:_____

BOOK:_____

CHAPTER:_____

BOOK:_____

CHAPTER:_____